FAMILY WORSHIP

BY STEVE DEMME

This book is dedicated to my ever supportive, always faithful, loving wife and my patient, forgiving, teachable sons who learned along with me.

May it bless the hearts of those men and women whose hearts God has touched to teach their children the Word of God.

BUILDINGFAITH
FAMILIES

Family Worship

FAMILY WORSHIP

BIG ROCKS

From an address given at a time management workshop

It was a packed house, and the noisy audience fell silent as the speaker walked to the platform carrying a two-gallon glass jar and plunked it down heavily on the lectern. From beneath the lectern he pulled out a pail filled with big rocks. Placing several of the large rocks in the glass jar until the last one was level with the top of the jar, he leaned into the microphone for the first time and in a booming voice asked, "Can anyone tell me if this jar is full?"

A voice near the front quickly replied, "If it won't hold any more rocks then it is full." The speaker responded, "Is it?" as he pulled out another pail from beneath the lectern that contained gravel. Pouring the gravel into the jar and shaking it into place around the big rocks, he once again asked, "Is the jar full now?"

Thinking they might have been the victims of a setup, the audience's only reply this time was a few chuckles and a general murmur of speculation.

"Aha, you're not so sure now, are you?" asked the speaker. "Well, how about now? Is it finally full?" he asked as he once again pulled out another pail and poured sand into the remaining space in the glass jar.

This time the audience was quick to toss out several affirmative retorts.

"Well now," said the speaker, "let's just check." This time he took out a pail of water and poured it into the glass jar. "Is it full now?" he asked one final time. This time there was no doubt, and the audience was united in its proclamation that the jar was indeed full.

"Well, you are quite right," said the speaker. "The jar is, in fact, completely 100 percent full. Now, can anyone tell me what the moral of this story is?"

From the center of the room a woman stood and, in a strong and confident voice, said, "If you were organized and planned well, you could always fit more activities into your day or week no matter how busy your schedule was." Now the audience was abuzz with general agreement when the speaker brought them back to reality by saying, "While that might be a very noble possibility, it is not the moral of this story. Does anyone else have any ideas?"

Following a few moments of relative silence, the speaker scanned the audience and said, "My dear friends, the moral of this story is this: if you don't get the big rocks in first, you won't get them in at all." He continued by saying, "In each of our lives we only have so much time. My challenge to you today is this: identify the big rocks in your life and make sure that you get them into the jar first each and every day."

For my wife Sandi and me, our big rock was to raise our children to live forever. Eternity is a long time. Perhaps a better word than raising our children is discipling our children. Discipleship has several components: prayer, modeling, and teaching. Only God can work in the heart of a child, but we believe it is our responsibility as parents to do our part and work with God by praying for their personal salvation, living out our faith in front of them, and teaching them the eternal Word of God.

For the Demme family, our daily Bible time was one of our big rocks. If you are interested in learning about the other ingredients of family discipleship, I have addressed living out or modeling your faith in several talks, which you may access on the web site www.buildingfaithfamilies.org.

I believe reading, studying, and meditating on God's Word is of paramount importance. Over the years, Sandi and I read many good books aloud to our children, but in our family devotion time we chose to read only Scripture.

"Heaven and earth will pass away, but my words will not pass away." (Matthew 24:35)

"All Scripture is breathed out by God and profitable for teaching, for reproof, for correction, and for training in righteousness, that the man of God may be complete, equipped for every good work." (2 Timothy 3:16–17)

We can't assume our children are going to receive a knowledge of God's inspired Word anywhere else. It is up to us as parents to teach and train our children. Others may come alongside for a time to support us, but they can never supplant us. No special training is needed to read the Bible. God wrote the Bible to be read by all of His people.

"For this commandment that I command you today is not too hard for you, neither is it far off. But the word is very near you. It is in your mouth and in your heart, so that you can do it." (Deuteronomy 30:11, 14)

Jesus was the Word made flesh. "In the beginning was the Word, and the Word was with God, and the Word was God. And the Word became flesh, and dwelt among us, and we have seen His glory, glory as of the only son from the Father, full of grace and truth." (John 1:1, 14)

In this short book I will be sharing what we did in our home to teach our children God's Word during our regular family worship time. I hope you will receive some ideas for your family time. While God's Word is eternal and His principles universal, how they are fleshed out will be different in every home since God has made each family to be unique.

The last few sections in the book will provide glimpses into other homes and how they have conducted family worship.

It doesn't say anywhere in scripture when you should teach, or how you should teach, or at what time of the day you should teach. I want to free you up as much as possible from any kind of condemnation you might feel because you don't do it like someone else. We are commanded to teach our children, but how, when, or what time, is not mentioned in scripture.

QUESTIONS FOR REFLECTION

1. What are your "Big Rocks"? List five.

2. Which ones change from year to year and which ones are lifelong?

3. What is your current plan for getting them into the jar first each day?

OUR RECIPE FOR FAMILY WORSHIP

Ingredient 1: Love God and His Word

Deuteronomy 6:7 is probably one of the most quoted Scripture references when speaking of teaching the Bible to your children. "You shall teach them diligently to your children, and shall talk of them when you sit in your house, and when you walk by the way, and when you lie down, and when you rise."

I thought of this verse many, many times as we raised our four sons, who are now all young men. I often pondered how to teach my sons as I sit, walk, lie down, and rise. Did this mean having regular family worship times? Did it mean memorizing Scripture and plastering our walls with Scripture?

In looking back, I see these are all worthwhile activities and this kind of thinking is correct, but I missed the order in which the Holy Spirit has orchestrated His Word. There is a reason verses 5 and 6 precede verse 7. Deuteronomy 6:5 says, "You shall love the Lord your God with all your heart and with all your soul and with all your might."

Before I can expect to teach my children the Word of God, I must be in a heart relationship with God myself. For the past year and a half I have been asking God to help me to love Him with all my heart, soul, mind, and strength.

I didn't know how He would answer this prayer, but since it is clearly according to His will, I knew He would. I expected I would wake up one morning and experience some sort of quickening in my heart and find my affections being drawn heavenward.

However the opposite happened. Instead of my feelings towards God changing, I have been increasingly aware of His affection for me.

Through a series of experiences and Scriptures, God has been teaching, revealing, and conveying to my heart how much He cares for me. Through these providences He has been communicating to me how much He loves and even likes me. I have chronicled this journey in a book entitled Knowing God's Love which was released in 2016.

As I pondered this, I realized this is consistent with how our heavenly Father operates. We read in 1 John 4:19 that "we love because he first loved us." As I have been shown how much God loves me, I am finding I love God more than ever.

My newfound appreciation for my Savior is in direct proportion to the revelation of His love for me. God has taken the initiative and made me know I am His and He is mine.

I never doubted God loved me because this truth is taught plainly in Scripture. However the verse which the Holy Spirit used to make me know how much He loved, and liked me, was John 15:9: "As the Father has loved Me, so have I loved You. Abide in My love." I can see how much God the Father loves Jesus, and to think Jesus loves me as much as His Father loves Him is incredible.

Deuteronomy 6:6 then says, "And these words that I command you today shall be on your heart." Years ago I was convicted as I read these words in Psalm 119:97 "Oh how I love your law! It is my meditation all the day."

I read the Bible regularly, but more from a sense of duty than from a love for the truth. I wanted to be able to say "Oh how I love your law!". I needed divine help to change of heart and enable me to love His word.

It was about this time I read this passage in Paul's epistle to the Thessalonians; "They received not the love of the truth, that they might be saved." (2 Thessalonians 2:10 ASV)

When I saw the word 'received' I thought of how I had received Jesus as my Savior, by asking in faith. I remembered how I had 'received' the gift of forgiveness by asking and believing. I knew it was God's will for me to love God and love His word, and I knew if we ask anything according to His will, God hears and answers our prayer (1 John 5:14-15).

I began asking God to give me grace to "love of the truth". God wonderfully answered and gave me the gift of loving truth. I now have God's word on my heart and can say with the Psalmist, "Oh how I love your law!" In fact Deuteronomy is now one my favorite books of the Bible and I look forward to reading this inspired book each year as I read through scripture.

The wisdom of the order of Deuteronomy 6:5-7 is amazing. When I love God and His Word, then I am equipped to teach the Word to my family. When God and His Word are the desire of my heart, talking about God and His words will flow from my heart and lips, when I rise up, walk by the way, lie down, and sit in my house.

When families are together 24 hours a day, 7 days a week, you have a chance to walk the talk. Parents have an opportunity to not only read the word of God but apply it in their lives in full view of the children. While hearing the inspired word of God is powerful, seeing it illustrated is wonderfully effective.

Not only do the children benefit by hearing and seeing the word, but parents benefit as well. Notice this fascinating passage, "When Enoch had lived 65 years, he fathered Methuselah. Enoch walked with God after he fathered Methuselah 300 years and had other sons and daughters. Thus all the days of Enoch were 365 years. Enoch walked with God, and he was not, for God took him." (Genesis 5:21-24)

We don't know all that went on in Enoch's heart, but it appears His life changed when he had a son. Perhaps being a father was the impetus he needed to draw near to God and set a godly example for his boy. We don't know, but Hebrews 11:5 says "Enoch was taken up so that he should not see death, and he was not found, because God had taken him. Now before he was taken he was commended as having pleased God."

I see with new eyes that the best thing I can do for my family is fall in love with God and His Word. A heart relationship with my heavenly Father is what prepares and equips me to teach my children.

This summer a friend sent me an email describing what God has been teaching him and his wife about home-based discipleship. With his permission I am sharing a few paragraphs with you:

"We are in a time of real soul-searching and transition of heart and mind from external-based, legalistic forms of 'family discipleship' to which we'd been exposed and thought, Well, that's how the so-called experts seem to be doing it. Our new goal is heart-based, humility-powered 'just loving each other.'

'Just loving each other' doesn't sound nearly as noble and high-minded as 'family discipleship,' but honestly it's what we need to do. We are desperate to see something of Jesus in our home these days."

Discipling our children is not a formula but a relationship. This relationship begins with our hearts as parents turning toward God and then toward home. May God save us from the external forms and appearances and do a deep work in our hearts which will birth relationships with God and each other that will last for eternity.

QUESTIONS FOR REFLECTION

1. What is the commandment in Deuteronomy 6:7?

2. What must we do before we can teach our children to love God and His word?

3. Consider watching a free video here, or reading Knowing God's Love.

Ingredient 2: God's Design for His Team

There are several ingredients for a positive experience with family worship. One of the most important is to recognize we are each a part of a team.

"Then the Lord God said, 'It is not good that the man should be alone; I will make him a helper fit for him.' So the Lord God caused a deep sleep to fall upon the man, and while he slept took one of his ribs and closed up its place with flesh. And the rib that the Lord God had taken from the man he made into a woman and brought her to the man. Then the man said, 'This at last is bone of my bones and flesh of my flesh; she shall be called Woman, because she was taken out of Man.' Therefore a man shall leave his father and his mother and hold fast to his wife, and they shall become one flesh." (Genesis 2:18, 21-24)

"Submitting to one another out of reverence for Christ. Wives, submit to your own husbands, as to the Lord." (Ephesians 5:21-22)

I believe scripture teaches the husband is the head of the home. I also believe God designed the husband and wife to be one flesh and function as a team to submit one to another as they instruct their children. The ideal home will have the dad and mom on the same page in this important arena of passing along truth to their kids. Much of this book is directed to the man, but I am thinking of both as I put pencil to paper. If your children are older, you may want to include them in the discussion.

Planning for the Parents

Here are some questions your "team" might consider before having your first worship experience at home. Planning will improve your experience. I would also suggest you take some time to discuss ways to tweak and improve your family worship times after you have met for a few days. This process is ongoing as children mature and your family dynamic changes from year to year.

"For which of you, desiring to build a tower, does not first sit down and count the cost, whether he has enough to complete it?" (Luke 14:28)

Here are some questions which may be beneficial for the "team" to discuss as they consider instituting regular family worship in their home.

1. When is the best time in the day to meet?
2. How many days per week will we be meeting?
3. Where is the best place to gather: the living room, kitchen, or dining room?
4. Who will lead the worship time if Dad is away from home? Is it possible to have devotions online with Dad?

For example, we aimed to meet together as soon as we finished breakfast, after the dishes were done and before our academic studies had commenced. Each weekday was our goal, and we met in the living room. Sandi led devotions when I was gone.

As you discuss with your wife when the best time . for devotions would be, remember she is probably the one spending most of the time with your kids, and she knows what works best with the regular family schedule already in place. It's not really fair for the husband to all of a sudden decide, "Hey, I heard this seminar about family devotions. I think this is something God wants me to do. How about tomorrow at 8:30 AM?" Be considerate. Communicate. Pray. You can always tweak the time and place depending on how it is going.

5.   Where will we begin our reading: Genesis, Matthew, or the Psalms?
6.   How much will we read each day: one verse or one chapter?
7.   Who will read: parents, children, or everyone?
8.   Do we need the same translation? (Either buy new Bibles or read a chapter on your computer and try different translations before purchasing.)
9.   What will we do for singing? In the section on Singing, Ingredient 12, I have listed some resources for families.
10. Do we want to memorize some psalms, hymns, and spiritual songs?
11. How will we manage the toddlers? Do we have some quiet toys, or paper, crayons, or markers for drawing?
12. When will we teach about forgiveness, conviction, and condemnation?
13. When would be the best time to pray and share answers to prayer? Each of these questions will be addressed as you continue to read.

Planning Helps the Whole Family

It's important to the children, as well as to you, to know what to expect in the daily devotions and how long they will go. You may have compliant kids who just take life in stride. But I received an email from a mom which offered some keen insight. She wrote, "My teenagers really struggled with family devotions. They didn't know when we were going to have them, and they didn't know how long they were going to go, because some days Dad got on a roll or one of his favorite subjects and went for 40 minutes. And other days we just met for five minutes. It was disconcerting to the kids since they didn't know what to expect. They didn't know if they were going to be called on to share or just listen."

They decided to institute a structure similar to what we did in our home, and it worked well for their family. The kids came to life and participated because there were no surprises and they knew what to expect. Find your own flavor, because what works for you might not work for me and vice versa.

Planning for Toddlers

Now when the kids were younger, I didn't mind if they played quietly while I was reading to them, as long as they weren't disruptive. There is a difference between semi-quiet playing and significant distraction. Remember the Golden Rule: do unto your children as you wish it would have been done unto you. I had trouble sitting still as a young boy. During church my mom would lean over as my knee bounced feverishly up and down and say, "You are shaking the whole pew!"

Children who are more than just a little antsy and need to learn how to sit quietly, are deposited in my lap. It's a lot easier to teach a child how to sit still when they're six than when they're sixteen. We've learned kids can learn to sit through a family worship time and eventually for a whole worship service at church. You might say, "Well, you've never seen my boy." I would ask if you have ever seen this same child stare at a video screen for an hour without moving? It's a question of motivation. I'm sure there are exceptions, but not as many as you may think.

QUESTIONS FOR REFLECTION

1. Read through the list of thirteen questions on pages 15–16 and determine which ones you are in agreement on a course of action. Mark the ones which require some planning and forethought and address them prayerfully.

2. When you are considering a structure for your first family devotion time, what will it look like?

3. If you have toddlers, what will be the best way to engage them?

Ingredient 3: Invite Jesus to Teach

The first thing we do after we are gathered together is pray. Jesus said, "For where two or three are gathered in my name, there am I among them." (Matthew 18:20) I like to invite Jesus to be present by His Spirit. There are a lot of Scriptures about asking.

"And I tell you, ask, and it will be given to you; seek, and you will find; knock, and it will be opened to you." (Luke 11:9)

When we gather our family together and invite God to teach us and meet with us, He does. As we draw near to Him, He draws near to us. He is the Good Shepherd, and He faithfully feeds His sheep. It is my responsibility to gather the sheep, but it is God's responsibility to feed them.

I learned this lesson while serving as a young pastor. I used to experience a good deal of stress on Saturday nights because I was serving a congregation who knew God a lot better than I did and for a lot longer than I had. I was young, fresh out of seminary, and I didn't feel like I really had much to share with them. My personal conviction is I don't like to talk about something unless I've applied it first, and I had a pretty limited experience file up to this point in my life.

Finally an older man took me aside and said, "Steve, look. God will feed His sheep. Do your homework and be diligent; ultimately He is the great Shepherd of those sheep, and He will feed them."

"But he who enters by the door is the shepherd of the sheep. To him the gatekeeper opens. The sheep hear his voice, and he calls his own sheep by name and leads them out. When he has brought out all his own, he goes before them, and the sheep follow him, for they know his voice." (John 10:2-4)

QUESTIONS FOR REFLECTION

1. Who will ultimately teach and feed the sheep?
2. Have you sensed the presence of God in your home when you have invited Him to be present?
3. How did Steve learn to rely on the Good Shepherd?

Ingredient 4: Begin in the Beginning

You may be wondering, Where should we begin? Genesis? Matthew? Proverbs? John? These are all great places. You could make a case for almost any of them. John was written "that you may believe that Jesus is the Christ, the Son of God, and that by believing you may have life in his name." (John 20:31) If you're focusing on salvation, read John.

I think you could make a pretty good case for starting with Genesis, since it's the first book. It's the beginning of THE Book. Isn't it funny we have to discuss this? Who's ever read a book by starting in the middle? Books were made to be read from the beginning.

I would like to make a case for the under-read and less-appreciated First Covenant, or Old Testament. I receive more personal applications reading the Old Testament than the New. In 1 Corinthians 10, Paul is talking about the children of Israel.

"For I do not want you to be unaware, brethren, that our fathers were all under the cloud, and all passed through the sea; and all were baptized into Moses in the cloud and in the sea. Now these things happened to them as an example, and they were written for our instruction, upon whom the ends of the ages have come." (1 Corinthians 10:1-2, 11)

God chose these factual accounts (they are not fictional stories) with us in mind. The Holy Spirit moved Moses and other writers to illustrate the truth for our generation.

How much do we know about Peter? He was brash and outspoken. He was a fisherman, and he was married, since Jesus cured his mother-in-law. We know a little more about Paul, a zealous Pharisee. We know much more about Abraham, Jacob, Joseph, and Moses. I feel like I know David, as I have read his prayer journal and watched him grow up as a youth, flee Saul, become king, and finally pass on as an old man who couldn't keep warm. God has used the life and person of David many times in my life.

Even though Saul is not a favorite persona, I identify with him. He was tall (as am I), and he fell because he feared the people. I share this temptation. Saul compromised; and Saul lost the kingdom. I am convicted every year when I read about Saul.

What about Solomon? He was the wisest man in the kingdom. As a king in Israel, he was given three commandments: "Only he must not acquire many horses for himself or cause the people to return to Egypt in order to acquire many horses, since the LORD has said to you, 'You shall never return that way again.' And he shall not acquire many wives for himself, lest his heart turn away, nor shall he acquire for himself excessive silver and gold." (Deuteronomy 17:16–17)

As you read through 1 Kings 10–11, you'll discover Solomon went down to Egypt for horses; silver and gold were like stones; and he had 700 wives and 300 concubines. Then it says, "and his heart was turned away." He was given three specific instructions, and he failed to obey each of them.

Maybe he felt he was so wise and mature these instructions no longer applied to him. Maybe he got lazy and didn't feel the need to keep reading Deuteronomy over and over. This speaks to me. I hope if you come visit me in a nursing home someday, I'll have these big, thick glasses, and I'll be reading through my large-print Bible every day. I am dead serious. I will never stop being a dependent child of God. I hope God will help me to mature in Christ, but I am never going to stop being His son. I will never become so smart I don't need to read my Bible.

Another reason I like to start at the beginning is because of a video called "*Ee-taow: The Mouk Story*," which is put out by New Tribes Mission (NTM). I recently watched this movie again at www.ntm.org. Ee-taow is the account of a missionary who went to Papua New Guinea. He was going to reach the people for Christ, and NTM decided to use a new method. Instead of learning the language then teaching about sin and salvation through Christ, they began a daily Bible study in Genesis and taught chronologically through the Old Testament for several months before mentioning Jesus.

During one class, the missionary, who had already taught about Abraham being the obedient friend of God and about God's blessing through Isaac, read about Isaac being bound on the sticks, with Abraham's knife poised. Then he said, "We'll pick this up tomorrow," and he stopped the class. What a great teaching technique! That evening, four different men in this Biblically illiterate culture came to the missionary independently and said, "God will provide a way of escape." The next day they learned God indeed provided a way of escape in the ram caught in the thicket. Several weeks later, when their study progressed to the death of Jesus, they understood Jesus was their ram in the thicket.

This was another confirmation to me that we should begin at the beginning, but pray together as a team and ask God to direct you where to begin.

"All Scripture is breathed out by God and profitable." (2 Timothy 3:16)

QUESTIONS FOR REFLECTION

1. Where will you begin reading the inspired words of God?
2. What is one advantage of beginning in Genesis?
3. What would one motivation be for beginning in John?

Ingredient 5: From Childhood

I'm a little bit of a zealot. When Isaac, my firstborn, was just a baby, I set aside time before church on Sunday mornings, sat on my bed with Isaac on my lap, and read the entire Book of Deuteronomy aloud. It took several Sundays, but I did it. I don't know what effect it had. I'm sure it didn't hurt him. From birthing classes, I'd heard about mothers talking to their babies in the womb and how babies in the womb can understand music and voices, so I thought, "I'm going to read him the Bible."

Jesus directs Peter to "Feed my lambs." (John 21:15)

Apparently Paul knew Timothy's family well because he says: "For I am mindful of the sincere faith within you, which first dwelt in your grandmother Lois, and your mother Eunice, and I am sure that it is in you as well." (2 Timothy 1:5)

Later, in the third chapter he comments on how old Timothy was when he began to learn the Scriptures: "From childhood you have been acquainted with the sacred writings, which are able to make you wise for salvation through faith in Christ Jesus." (2 Timothy 3:15)

Children are astute. They hear things and believe what they hear.

Fat

Isaac was four, Ethan was two, and we had just finished eating dinner. My wife and I got up and were walking around when we overheard the boys having a discussion with some intensity. We peeked around the corner so they wouldn't know we were watching. Ethan was innocently looking at Isaac and asking,

"Why?", and Isaac said, "Don't eat that," referring to the gravy and meat on Ethan's plate. Ethan looked up with his innocent blue eyes and said, "Why not?" Isaac responded authoritatively, "The fat belongs to Jehovah!"

I'm not going to take personal responsibility for this story. I don't recall ever teaching this as doctrine, but somewhere along the line, sitting in a worship service or hearing somebody read the Bible, Isaac had heard the fat belongs to God. He not only believed it; he was applying it!

Harlots

We have another friend who thought harlots were musical instruments, since Israel was always "playing the harlot!"

Since kids are so bright and impressionable, it is good to read them the Word of God when they are young. God chose to reveal Himself in the written word. He didn't create movies on DVDs. He didn't choose Charlton Heston, although it is hard to read Exodus without seeing Charlton Heston standing with outstretched arms as the Red Sea parts. God didn't choose these visual means. He chose to write the words. They're meant to be read.

Before our sons were able to read the Bible themselves, we read Scripture to them. In those early years, we liked to read from the *The Bible Story*, by Arthur S. Maxwell (Uncle Arthur). There are ten volumes with pictures. I found them remarkably accurate, although I disagree with some of the theology in the last volume. They are pricey new, but we found ours used and affordable.

When we did read Scripture to them, we used discernment and read what we thought was appropriate for their age. We avoided gruesome parts like the concubine being carved up into pieces and sent throughout the twelve tribes at the end of Judges. Use your best judgment in what to read and when to read it.

QUESTIONS FOR REFLECTION

1. When did Timothy learn the scriptures and from whom?

2. Recall one instance where your children surprised you with their ability to understand truth?

3. How old do children need to be to participate in Bible reading?

Ingredient 6: Read

After we pray, we take turns reading aloud around the room. Once our boys were able to read for themselves, I purchased large print Bibles, in the same version, so we could all read from the same translation. This was our practice for several years, but we go through seasons. After the boys went to Bible school and college, we would have several different versions being read as we proceeded around the room.

We focused on one chapter per day. We have six people in our family: Sandi and I, Isaac, Ethan, Joseph, and John. When we first got started we experimented with how many verses each person would read. One verse per turn didn't work for our family because it was moving too quickly from reader to reader, and it was difficult to listen since you wanted to make sure you didn't miss your turn when it was coming back around the circle. We tried reading as many as four or five verses at a time, but some fell asleep waiting for their turn. Two or three verses per reader worked well for our home.

We did go through the math phase for a while. If there were fifteen verses and six people, then each person read two and half verses. My wife would roll her eyes, so we stopped this adventure, but the boys and I got a kick out of it.

For a while I timed our reading and found it took about 8.3 minutes to read a chapter of Scripture. It doesn't take long, unless you are reading Psalm 119.

My reasoning for reading aloud is found in two places in Scripture:

"Until I come, devote yourself to the public reading of Scripture, to exhortation, to teaching." (1 Timothy 4:13)

"Blessed is the one who reads aloud the words of this prophecy, and blessed are those who hear, and who keep what is written in it, for the time is near." (Revelation 1:3)

Reading, as well as hearing, makes learning more effective. We discovered even when we didn't comprehend every verse we read with our minds, our spirits were still being cleansed and nurtured.

"Already you are clean because of the word that I have spoken to you." (John 15:3)

"That He might sanctify her, having cleansed her by the washing of water with the Word." (Ephesians 5:26)

While we were reading, we encouraged each other to pause at commas and enunciate Ts and Ds at the ends of words. This is a good opportunity to practice reading clearly and accurately.

Everyone had a turn, even those who have difficulty reading. Our fourth son has Down syndrome and can only read a limited number of words, but he wants to have his turn like everyone else, and we quickly learned not to skip him or we would hear about it. He keeps his Bible open and when it is his turn will "read". He always knows when it's his turn. He frequently reminds his older brother, who will remain nameless, when it is time to read. Have fun in your reading and include everyone who wants to participate. This is your family; enjoy them.

We attempted to read the entire Bible from Genesis to Revelation together. There are a few minor prophets we didn't finish. Maybe some day we will accomplish this on one of our family vacations or when we are gathered all together for a holiday.

If we just read our favorite portions, we won't be getting a balanced diet. We might gravitate to Galatians, but we know we need Deuteronomy as well.

"Man shall not live by bread alone, but by every word that comes from the mouth of God." (Matthew 4:4)

Some may ask which method of Bible study we used: inductive or deductive. We used the "read" method. Even though I am aware of different techniques for digging deeper into the Word of God, and all have merit, I wanted my sons to at least have read the book before they examined it in greater detail.

"The sum of Thy Word is truth, and every one of Thy righteous ordinances is everlasting." (Psalm 119:160 NASB)

Many students I attended seminary with had never read the Bible from cover to cover. At this point in my life, neither had I, yet I was taking classes in theology. I didn't know enough Scripture to know if what I was being taught was true or not. I didn't even know what questions to ask because I was biblically illiterate.

I do think there is a point where it is helpful to dig deeper and do word studies and consider doctrines such as the deity of Christ, the trinity, and justification by faith, but only after a broad groundwork of Scripture has been laid. I didn't want to teach a form of theology and fit the Scriptures into this framework. I sought to promote a broad base of biblical knowledge and then examine theology in light of the Word.

"Now these Jews were more noble than those in Thessalonica; they received the word with all eagerness, examining the Scriptures daily to see if these things were so." (Acts 17:11)

When your children are younger, read to them. When your children are older, read with them.

QUESTIONS FOR REFLECTION

1. Of the two verses which motivated Steve's family to read aloud, which one speaks to your heart and why?

2. Do people need to understand the word of God fully to benefit from hearing it? Why?

3. What are the implications of Matthew 4:4?

Ingredient 7: Look for Jesus

There are many reasons to read the Bible, but a wonderful fruit from daily searching the scriptures is receiving new glimpses of Jesus. "You search the Scriptures because you think that in them you have eternal life; and it is they that bear witness about me," (John 5:39) for these words of life reveal the Son of God, who is the central character in Scripture.

Before you commence reading, consider asking God's Spirit to open your eyes to see Jesus. "When the Helper comes, whom I will send to you from the Father, the Spirit of truth, who proceeds from the Father, he will bear witness about me." (John 15:26) I like the request of certain Greeks to Philip in John 12:21: "Sir, we would see Jesus."

If I could go to Whit's End in Odyssey (Adventures in Odyssey is an original audio series produced by Focus on the Family), I would go into the time machine and ask to be a witness to one of the greatest Bible studies of all time. It took place on the road to Emmaus, after the crucifixion of our Savior. Cleopas and a friend were walking along the road, commiserating about the events of the past few days, when Jesus joined them and began to walk with them. He then began to teach them from the Scriptures.

"And beginning with Moses and all the Prophets, he interpreted to them in all the Scriptures the things concerning Himself." (Luke 24:27)

Recently I was reading in my personal devotions the first chapter of Leviticus. I do not look forward to reading this book as much as others, but I know it is inspired and profitable, so I read it annually, as well as the rest of the Bible. Before I began, I asked the Holy

Spirit if He would help me see Jesus in the reading for this day.

"If his offering is a burnt offering from the herd, he shall offer a male without blemish. He shall bring it to the entrance of the tent of meeting, that he may be accepted before the LORD. He shall lay his hand on the head of the burnt offering, and it shall be accepted for him to make atonement for him." (Leviticus 1:3-4)

I knew Jesus was the male without defect, but what I saw for the first time was the instruction to "lay his hand on the head of the burnt offering." Immediately I thought of Jesus directing the hand of Thomas to lay his hand on Him. Tears welled up in my eyes as I thought of Jesus in this new light.

"Put your finger here, and see my hands; and put out your hand, and place it in my side. Do not disbelieve, but believe." (John 20:27)

QUESTIONS FOR REFLECTION

1. Who reveals Jesus in the word?

2. Where is Jesus in Leviticus?

3. Where have you seen Jesus in scripture outside of the four gospels?

Ingredient 8: Do Unto Others, or The Golden Rule

See if you can recall what it was like to be school age. Do you remember your favorite teachers? What made them special? This exercise may help you to teach your students the way you liked being taught. I liked having fun at that age (and still do). I enjoyed illustrations. Jesus called them parables. Perhaps you have had some training and experience as a Sunday school teacher, youth group leader, or vacation Bible school instructor. Use the insights you have gained in teaching children, along with any fun games you have played.

Here's one game most of you may know which I learned while working with young people: sword drill. Since the Bible is the sword of the Spirit, everyone holds their Bible in the air while the leader calls out a reference. This is the signal for everyone to begin searching for that specific Scripture. The first one to find it stands and reads it aloud. Then all "sheath their swords" and the leader picks another one (or you can have the winner choose the next verse).

I learned another edifying and fun activity I'll call the Read-Along Game. Let's assume in our family devotion time we're studying John, which has 21 chapters. If we read three or four chapters per week, it might take us a month and a half to read through this book. During the first week, when we are in the first four chapters, I open to a passage and begin reading aloud. The first person to locate where I am reading and read along with me is the "victor." Now it is their turn to read from one of these four chapters. As the adrenaline of competition kicks in, I find myself listening intently for key words while I am scanning Scripture, and in the course of the game become more familiar with God's Word.

We made up some new rules as we went along. When we first began a new section of Scripture, we had each person begin reading at the beginning of a chapter. When we got more familiar with this portion, we then announced you could start anywhere in the chapter. To encourage the younger kids, we said you couldn't win twice in a game until everybody had a chance to win once. Do whatever works for your home. Bottom line: teach like you would have liked to have been taught. Learning can be fun.

These first few ideas make learning fun, but there is more to the principle of the Golden Rule than edutainment. Put yourself in the shoes of each of your children. Students don't just want to have a good time; they have other needs, like being valued and respected. I learned a lot from my son who has Down Syndrome. He wants to be treated just like his siblings. He wants to be heard, and have a voice. He wants to be included. He knows when he is being patronized, which is discouraging to him, as it is to any of us. If we value each person in the family and treat them as we want to be treated, the message we are conveying to their hearts goes beyond the content of the Scripture we are studying. We are communicating they too have been created in the image of God.

I'm an old guy now, but if there was one area I would change as I look back at our family dynamic, I would work much harder to provide a home environment where the atmosphere was safe. Where each person was free to hold and express their own opinion whether I agreed or not. Where we treated each other respectfully and believed the best of each other. When we studied the Scriptures and discussed what we were reading, I would aim for an atmosphere where no one was squelched or cut off because it was the minority opinion. Good, honest, clear communication provides the basis for healthy family relationships.

QUESTIONS FOR REFLECTION

1. Who was your favorite teacher wen you were in school or Sunday school? Why?

2. What is the most fun and effective way for you to learn scripture?

3. Do your children feel safe to ask any question or make any comment in your home?

Ingredient 9: As I Have Loved You

The greatest command, according to Jesus, is Matthew 22:7: "You shall love the Lord your God with all your heart and with all your soul and with all your mind." Then Jesus says the second command is to love your neighbor as yourself. I noticed this past year in John 13, Jesus gives what He calls a new commandment: "A new commandment I give to you, that you love one another: just as I have loved you, you also are to love one another" verse 34. I have pondered these words and what it means for me to love others as Jesus has loved me. In the context of this book I think of two applications.

The first is of Jesus taking the form of a servant. "Have this mind among yourselves, which is yours in Christ Jesus, who, though he was in the form of God, did not count equality with God a thing to be grasped, but emptied himself, by taking the form of a servant" (Philippians 2:5-7). "You know that the rulers of the Gentiles lord it over them, and their great ones exercise authority over them. It shall not be so among you. But whoever would be great among you must be your servant, and whoever would be first among you must be your slave, even as the Son of Man came not to be served but to serve, and to give his life as a ransom for many" (Matthew 20:25-28).

As a dad and husband, I am the leader of the home, but as a Christian dad, this means I am NOT to be the lord but the servant. This is how Jesus loved me. He could have lorded it over me, for He is Lord of lords and King of kings, but instead He chose to wash my feet and lay His life down for me. Paul asserted as an apostle, he had "the authority that the

Lord has given me for building up and not for tearing down" (2 Corinthians 13:10). If I have this mindset I will be building up and serving, not lording over or tearing down.

The second area is one which I am working hard on even now, not quenching the spirit of my wife or children. "Behold, my servant whom I have chosen, my beloved with whom my soul is well pleased.... He will not quarrel or cry aloud... a bruised reed he will not break, and a smoldering wick he will not quench" (Matthew 12:18-20). Regardless of how old my sons are, I will always be their dad, who has the power to build them up like no one else and the power to hurt or quench their spirits like no one else. I know it might only be a look or a sarcastic comment, BUT I have the potential to wound those who are closest to me. I would rather be an encourager and a lifelong supporter of my family, as Jesus is to me.

QUESTIONS FOR REFLECTION

1. What is the first and great commandment? Does this sound similar to Deuteronomy 6:5?

2. What is the "New" commandment in your own words?

3. What is the essence of Matthew 20:25-28?

Ingredient 10: Exhort One Another

"Therefore encourage one another and build one another up, just as you are doing" (1 Thessalonians 5:11).

If we have time after singing, we will go around the room and share insights from the morning reading. I might prime the pump by asking, "What did you hear today? What did you learn? What stood out to you in today's Bible reading?" It's always amazing to me how different people can read the same passage of Scripture and receive different insights. It's edifying to hear other people's testimonies. Everyone has something to offer.

"As each has received a gift, use it to serve one another, as good stewards of God's varied grace:" (1 Peter 4:10).

Children's contributions are not just "cute"; often they have valuable observations. Esteem the wisdom of each member of the family. The leader of the meeting does not have to talk the most or force his opinions on everyone else. Harsh, dominating tones exasperate our children and provoke them to anger, both of which parents are forewarned not to do. My job as facilitator and teacher is to ask good questions, give an answer for the hope which I hold, and allow room for the Holy Spirit to have free course in my own heart. A godly leader creates an atmosphere where each person is free to share what they have learned and what is on their heart.

This is a wonderful opportunity to encourage children to articulate what they have learned so they can edify others. A godly man once remarked, "Impression without expression can lead to depression." He likened this to the Sea of Galilee, which is always giving. It nourishes the land of Israel with its fresh living water. The Salt Sea is always receiving and, as a result, becomes the Dead Sea.

"What then, brothers? When you come together, each one has a hymn, a lesson, a revelation, a tongue, or an interpretation. Let all things be done for building up" (1 Corinthians 14:26).

I have always held the conviction that a disciple is a lifelong learner. As a parent, I have a few years' head start in following Jesus, but while God has called me to lead my family, I am also a co-learner. I may be the oldest, but this does not imply I know all the answers. May God grant me and all parents a humble, teachable spirit like the man in Isaiah and the tax-gatherer in Luke 18. "But the tax-gatherer, standing some distance away, was even unwilling to lift up his eyes to heaven, but was beating his breast, saying, 'God, be merciful to me, the sinner!' "I tell you, this man went down to his house justified rather than the other; for everyone who exalts himself shall be humbled, but he who humbles himself shall be exalted" (Luke 18:13-14 NASB). "But to this one I will look, To him who is humble and contrite of spirit, and who trembles at My word" (Isaiah 66:2 NASB).

A teachable disciple is also not looking around the room when the Bible is being read and thinking how some particular truths apply to other members of the family. A humble co-learner instead says, "What saith my Lord to me?" I have adapted a section of Matthew 7 which is helpful to me along this line. "And why do you look at the speck that is in your child's eye, but do not notice the log that is in your own eye? Or how can you say to your child, 'Let me take the speck out of your eye,' and behold, the log is in your own eye? You hypocrite, first take the log out of your own eye, and then you will see clearly to take the speck out of your child's eye" (Matthew 7:3-5).

QUESTIONS FOR REFLECTION

1. Who has a spiritual gift and what is the purpose of these gifts?

2. Recall one example where a child has edified you with their insight?

3. Before we correct our children, what is our first responsibility according to Matthew 7?

Ingredient 11: Grace and Truth

"For the law was given through Moses; grace and truth came through Jesus Christ." John 1:17

"Loving kindness and truth have met together; righteousness and peace have kissed each other." Psalm 85:10 NASB

Jesus was the perfect blend of truth given with grace and grace mixed with truth. As I teach, read God's Word, and share insights in our devotion time, I try to remember to share the good news of grace and forgiveness with myself and my family. We all need grace along with truth. God's forgiveness and grace are not only for salvation when we first believe but throughout our lives. We are saved by grace, and we live by grace.

After hearing me present this message on family worship at a conference, a lady came to the front and introduced herself by saying she worked in a drug rehabilitation center. She told me that many of the people in the center were children of fundamentalist Christian parents. I asked her what she thought the connection was. She believed that these adults had never been taught how to process guilt when they were children. They didn't know how to receive forgiveness. She explained that drugs and alcohol were a form of self-inflicted punishment, or a kind of slow suicide. They knew that they were guilty and were punishing themselves.

As children hear the truth, they will experience conviction, which can lead to guilt since they have a tender conscience. This is a critical time to explain the forgiveness that only Jesus can extend since He died to take away our sins on the cross. He had no sins of His own, and so He could take ours upon Himself.

"Behold, the Lamb of God, who takes away the sin of the world!" John 1:29

"For our sake he made him to be sin who knew no sin, so that in him we might become the righteousness of God." 2 Corinthians 5:21

When we confess our sins, He forgives them and takes them away.

"If we confess our sins, he is faithful and just to forgive us our sins and to cleanse us from all unrighteousness." 1 John 1:9

"As far as the east is from the west, so far has He removed our transgressions from us." Psalm 103:12

If we've offended another person, we need to ask their forgiveness as well.

"Then Peter came up and said to him, 'Lord, how often will my brother sin against me, and I forgive him? As many as seven times?' Jesus said to him, 'I do not say to you seven times, but seventy times seven.'" Matthew 18:21-22

If one of the family members struggles with God's grace and forgiveness, this may be a good time to introduce them to Psalm 51, which is David's prayer after his heinous sin with Bathsheba.

This is also a wonderful opportunity to teach your children the difference between conviction and condemnation. These are big words, but they are the difference between life and death. Conviction, or godly sorrow, as described in 2 Corinthians, leads to repentance, which leads to life. Worldly grief, or condemnation, leads to death.

"For godly grief produces a repentance that leads to salvation without regret, whereas worldly grief produces death." 2 Corinthians 7:10

Peter was convicted (godly grief) when he denied Jesus.

"And Peter remembered the saying of Jesus, 'Before the rooster crows, you will deny me three times.' And he went out and wept bitterly." Matthew 26:75

Peter was helped to get his eyes back onto Jesus, received forgiveness, and became a pillar of the early church. I would like to have heard Peter preach a sermon of forgiveness of sin. I doubt if he ever did so without remembering how Jesus had extended grace and reconciliation to him.

On the other hand, Judas was condemned (worldly grief) when faced with his sin, which led to despair, and he went out and hanged himself.

"Then when Judas, his betrayer, saw that Jesus was condemned, he changed his mind and brought back the thirty pieces of silver to the chief priests and the elders, saying, 'I have sinned by betraying innocent blood.' They said, 'What is that to us? See to it yourself.' And throwing down the pieces of silver into the temple, he departed, and he went and hanged himself." Matthew 27:3–5

Children have tender consciences, and they believe what they hear. Look at family devotions from their perspective. As parents, you are carving time out of your busy schedule and devoting it to studying God's Word. As they read and hear the Word of God, they believe the truth and earnestly seek to apply it. Even if you are reading the New Testament, what is being taught can come across as law. These encounters with truth that produce conviction are opportunities to come to Jesus.

"The law is become our tutor to bring us unto Christ, that we might be justified by faith." Galatians 3:24

A wise pastor once commented that all sermons should end at the cross. Come to Jesus for forgiveness regularly. He always extends grace and forgiveness.

"Come to me, all who labor and are heavy laden, and I will give you rest. Take my yoke upon you, and learn from me, for I am gentle and lowly in heart, and you will find rest for your souls. For my yoke is easy, and my burden is light." Matthew 11:28–30

I recently spoke about family discipleship at a church in Ohio. On Sunday morning, the lady that organized it came up to me and said, "Steve, I have a story to tell you. This morning my oldest daughter, about nine, came to me with tears in her eyes and said, 'Mama, sometimes I call you names in my head.'" She was convicted because she'd heard me talk about this subject the day before. She asked her mother to forgive her, and they had a wonderful time of going to the cross together. When I saw the girl in church, she was glowing because she'd been forgiven and relieved of her burden. If this dear girl hadn't been sitting in the meetings with her family, she would still be carrying this load of guilt. Children listen and understand.

QUESTIONS FOR REFLECTION

1. Which scripture concerning forgiveness is worthy of being memorized?

2. What is the difference between conviction and condemnation?

3. The law was given through Moses; _____ and _____ came through Jesus Christ.

Ingredient 12: Make a Joyful Noise

"Make a joyful noise to the LORD, all the earth! Serve the LORD with gladness! Come into his presence with singing!" (Psalm 100:1-2)

If we had time in the morning, we might sing after we had read from the Bible. There were several factors which contributed to what we chose to sing. I realized early on our repertoire as a family was very limited. On one errand when we were all together in the car, I said, "Let's sing all of the gospel songs we know." In a few minutes it was quiet. We knew "Only a Boy Named David," "The Wise Man Built His House upon the Rock," and a few first verses of hymns,and some Christmas carols, but this was the extent of our knowledge.

About the same time we attended a seminar where we were encouraged to memorize hymns. I also recalled Elisabeth Elliot sharing how the Holy Spirit used hymns she had learned in her youth to encourage her through the many valley experiences in her life. She mentioned her parents would gather the family together before school each morning, sing one hymn, and read one chapter of Scripture. I also was influenced by the Book of Acts. If I were ever in prison with Paul and Silas, I wouldn't be able to contribute much to the singing of hymns from memory!

One of my favorite books and movies is Pollyanna. She and her dad used to play the Glad Game after he searched the Scriptures one night and discovered over 800 "glad" verses. I looked up the following words with my concordance to see how many times they are mentioned in the Bible: praise—210, joy—173, joyful—26, sing—126, song—82, worship—103, rejoice—179,

gladness—46, give thanks—58. Together we have 921
"glad" references.

Scripture and praise go together. In the recent
history of the church, we have preachers of the
gospel accompanied by song leaders. Billy Graham
and George Beverly Shea ministered together. Before
them we had D. L. Moody as the evangelist and Ira
Sankey leading the worship. P. P. Bliss worked with
R. A. Torrey. Worship and the Word complement
each other.

"Let the high praises of God be in their throats and
two-edged swords in their hands." (Psalm 149:6)

I am drawn to hymns which have stood the test of
time, especially those rich in Scripture and theology. In
my personal valleys, when life is tough, and God seems
distant, it is then my theology and what I know about
God kicks in. The knowledge of God acquired through
singing and memorizing hymns helps me through
these dark days when I have little or no inspiration.

Elisabeth Elliot's family (the Howards) would go
through a hymn book in a year. Number 1, January 1.
Number 2, January 2. However, they had a pianist in the
home. In order for our family to sing in our home, I had
to contract with a friend to record piano accompaniment
on cassettes. We bought several hymnals, started with
number 1 in January, and over a period of two years
sang almost 200 songs. It was a rich experience.

For a season we decided to memorize hymns. We
discovered our children learned verses much more
quickly than we did. After singing a verse through
two or three times, the kids were already on their
way to picking it up. As parents, we are the ones who
struggled, but we did have the advantage of having

heard these hymns many times over the years. Since we have boys, and boys are more visual, we used to pass out a piece of paper, markers, and crayons and encourage them to draw a picture of the verse we were studying. We focused on one verse for a day or two until we all knew it by heart.

Sometimes we had hymns which were difficult to illustrate. In "Dare to Be a Daniel," the first verse is "standing by a purpose firm, heeding God's command." How do you illustrate a purpose firm? Do you know what we did? A dead porpoise. After rigor mortis sets in, you have a "porpoise firm". This was all I could come up with. The boys loved it. "Oh, yeah dead fish!" My wife just rolled her eyes and smiled benignly upon her children—all five of them.

I've forgotten most of the props and the pictures, but I have memorized several hymns now. If I'm ever in prison, I can now contribute; I've got nine hymns under my belt.

For those of you who are interested in singing hymns in your home, I developed a resource called Hymns for Family Worship, with 100 hymns, four (4) CDs of piano accompaniment, along with the history of each hymn. On page 105 there is a one page description of this resource. You may order them at http://store. demmelearning.com/catalog/building-faith-families and find them in the Store.

"Let the word of Christ dwell in you richly, teaching and admonishing one another in all wisdom, singing psalms and hymns and spiritual songs, with thankfulness in your hearts to God." (Colossians 3:16)

QUESTIONS FOR REFLECTION

1. What are some benefits of singing?

2. Which verse in the Bible confirms scripture and praise go together?

3. How might you incorporate praise and worship in your home?

Ingredient 13: Reminisce

Share your experiences with your family. Don't assume they know all God has done in your life. Tell your kids how you got saved and how you met your wife. Share answers to prayer. One Saturday night after a conference, I had dinner with one of the vendors. With four boys and one daughter, I asked mom and dad to tell me how they came to Christ and met each other.

I knew they both spoke Spanish, but I didn't know where they were from. I found out they met in Miami, but she was from Ecuador, and he was from Colombia. It was a wonderful testimony, but what blessed me the most was how their kids kept interrupting, "Hey, don't forget that point, Mom! Hey, Dad, tell them about when you ..." They were enjoying the story! It was a beautiful picture.

"One generation shall commend your works to another, and shall declare your mighty acts." (Psalm 145:4)

One of my significant life experiences happened when I prayed for a pair of boots. I had been reading powerful biographies about Hudson Taylor, George Mueller, and Jim Elliott. These men prayed for their physical needs to be met without asking people to help them. When George Mueller needed food for his orphanage, he prayed instead of asking churches in the city. Over and over, God miraculously would answer their prayers. These books made a huge impression on me, and I wondered if God would answer my prayers and meet my needs as He had met their needs.

During my college and seminary years I painted houses during the summer. I'd buy a pair of work boots and wear them through the winter for the snow and slush; then in the summer I'd use them for painting. I went through a pair of boots every year, and since it was October I was in need of a new pair for the winter. Because I had been hearing about praying for my needs, I decided to ask God for a pair of boots.

That fall, my mom and dad came up to visit. We went shopping in Gloucester, Massachusetts. I wasn't very interested and was waiting by the door in one shop when I noticed a large wire mesh barrel, about three feet high, filled with footwear. I went over, found a pair of large work boots near the top, and checked the size. Size 13—they fit! The price was one dollar! I could hardly believe it. Those work boots meant more to me than all of George Mueller's bread which he prayed for the orphans in London, because God heard my little prayer for a pair of boots. I kept those boots for years. I even kept one on the mantel in our living room after I wore them out. (My wife and I still debate over who threw it away.)

Don't only share your own experiences; keep your children's experiences fresh as well. Many children in Christian homes come to Jesus at an early age. Help them keep this memory fresh. Over the years I've ministered to adults who think, "I don't remember what happened when I was young," and they are tempted to doubt if they were really saved.

My wife is making scrapbooks for each of our sons. She told them when they were young she was planning on doing this, and they have gathered memorabilia for many years. I was at my second son's house the other night, reading through his scrapbook, and there was his testimony in pencil which he'd written when he was six or seven years old. He told how he came to Jesus and was baptized. Sandi had put together a picnic to commemorate this significant event. She chose a red tablecloth to represent the blood of Jesus and spread it out in the backyard. It was a special time.

Then there was the time Joseph and I were going to buy some apples in Ipswich. As we were talking, he made a comment about his being a Christian, and I thought, "Well, maybe this is the moment." I said, "Actually, Jose, none of us are born God's children. We all have to be adopted because we are all born sinners." I explained the gospel the best I could to a five-year-old and asked if he would like to receive Jesus. He did. We prayed together in the car, on the way to the orchard. On the way home, he began processing what had transpired and asked, "When I jump on the trampoline, will Jesus go up and down too?" He knew Jesus had come into his heart, and he was picturing Jesus in his heart bouncing when he bounced! It was real to him that Jesus had come to live in his heart.

All of these experiences are blessed times, and it helps me to remember them as I write. I hope you will find blessing as you discover ways to keep these sacred experiences alive for your family.

When I was working as a pastor, God began to convict me about giving my family the first fruits instead of the crumbs. This might not be a problem to you, but it was for me. One night I received a really good insight about Jesus, and my first thought was, "This will make a great sermon." Then the Holy Spirit whispered, "What about your family?" So for devotions the next day, I shared this insight. Later God led me to use it as a sermon, but I was learning family comes first.

Share dreams! Debbie, a good friend of mine, had a dream of the Lord's return. In her dream, Jesus was coming back in the clouds. If you know Debbie, you know she loves Jesus. She has a special relationship with her Savior. When she saw Him returning, she had to get to Him. She began to run, and the next thing she knew, she was in the clouds. Off to one side she saw her pastor coming at an angle from his side of town. Now, Debbie is five feet something, and her pastor is over six feet tall and used to run track in school. He was moving smoothly with big, long, loping strides, but she zoomed right past him.

It made such an impression on the whole congregation that she was asked to relate her dream in church. Later she wrote it for inclusion in the church publication. Two years later, I had two of her children in Sunday School studying the second coming, and I asked them, "Do you remember the dream your mom had about the Lord's return?" They said, "What dream?" Her own family had never heard it.

We have this tendency to share experiences in church and write them out for the church magazine instead of passing them along to our families. May God help us to have our priorities in the proper order.

QUESTIONS FOR REFLECTION

1. Have your children ever heard your testimony of how you came to faith in Jesus?

2. Can you think of a time when God wonderfully answered prayer for you?

3. Have your children ever written out their own salvation experience?

Ingredient 14: Your Family History

The word remember, or a form of it such as remembrance, is found in over 200 verses in Scripture. Here are a few examples.

"On that night the king could not sleep. And he gave orders to bring the book of memorable deeds, the chronicles, and they were read before the king." (Esther 6:1)

"And you shall remember the whole way that the LORD your God has led you these forty years in the wilderness, that he might humble you, testing you to know what was in your heart, whether you would keep his commandments or not." (Deuteronomy 8:2)

Keeping a record of your progress, what chapters you have read, and what days you did meet will be a source of encouragement for those days when you are tempted to be discouraged. Looking at the glass of water as half full and not half empty is much more encouraging. Instead of lamenting over the days you did not meet together, be grateful for the ones you did. If you have one devotion a month this year, this may be twelve more than last year!

Perhaps you could assign the task of chronicling your family's progress to one of the children. His or her title could be Jehoshaphat. Or you could rotate the responsibility among all members of the family.

"Joab the son of Zeruiah was over the army; and Jehoshaphat the son of Ahilud was recorder." (1 Chronicles 18:15)

Many years ago our family began recording what we were thankful for on a weekly basis. Each Friday we had what we called a "Thanks Service." We went around the room, and each person had an opportunity to think back over the previous seven days of what they were grateful to God for. After over twenty years, this written record has grown into a small stack of spiral bound notebooks which has become a precious history of our home.

We reminded ourselves, "Every good gift and every perfect gift is from above, coming down from the Father of lights with whom there is no variation or shadow due to change." (James 1:17)

We practiced giving thanks for all things and not just the "blessings," or the good things, as we perceived them.

"Give thanks in all circumstances; for this is the will of God in Christ Jesus for you." (1 Thessalonians 5:18)

If I could have picked a family in Israel to be born into, it would have been the family of Asaph. What a great job, to continually look for ways to be thankful.

"On that day David first assigned Asaph and his relatives to give thanks to the LORD." (1 Chronicles 16:7 NASB)

QUESTIONS FOR REFLECTION

1. What did the Demme's weekly 'Thanks Service' look like?

2. How do you record significant family events in your family?

3. How do you help each other remember what God has done for your home?

Ingredient 15: Close with Prayer

Since we begin our worship time asking God to meet us as we draw near to Him, it is good to thank Him for being with us. I like to wrap up our meetings by thanking God for visiting and teaching us and then committing all which has been read, said, and sung to God in prayer.

"Commit your way to the LORD; trust in him, and he will act." (Psalm 37:5)

"Commit your work to the LORD, and your plans will be established." (Proverbs 16:3)

You may also want to take this time to ask if there are any needs for prayer.

"In everything by prayer and supplication with thanksgiving let your requests be made known to God." (Philippians 4:6)

QUESTIONS FOR REFLECTION

1. Why pray at the end of a family worship time?

2. Who will be responsible to pray?

3. Could you take turns praying?

Ingredient 16: Just Do It

We will examine all of the potential obstacles I can think of in the next section of the book, but here is when I put on my Nike hat and say "Just do it." And here's the Scripture for Nike:

"Open your mouth wide and I will fill it." (Psalm 81:10)

When I first began leading our family worship times I was inspired and convicted, but my inspiration and conviction faded. I have trouble with discipline and follow through. My wife is the steady one on our team. She plans her work and works her plan. She has the calendar of the Persians and the Medes (whose laws could not be altered) which she faithfully follows. Under my shaky leadership our worship times were not regular; we would do well for several weeks, and then have none for a few weeks. Something would happen, or someone would get sick, or perhaps work would pile up. Realizing I had dropped the ball led to me being discouraged, then I would get my courage up and try it one more time. Even though I was not consistent, we kept at it. One of the most encouraging Scriptures to me as a dad is Proverbs 24:16, which says, "The righteous falls seven times and rises again".

By God's grace I kept getting up and trying again. Eventually, family devotions became a habit in our home, but it did take a few years. A friend of mine once observed every time someone gets back on their feet after being down, it is a mini-resurrection. Even though I may not recognize His help, every time I get up it is God's Spirit helping me to my feet.

"If the Spirit of him who raised Jesus from the dead dwells in you, he who raised Christ Jesus from the dead will also give life to your mortal bodies through his Spirit who dwells in you." (Romans 8:11).

So how do we get started? We pray, consult with our teammate and spouse, and do it. Somebody has to sit down and gather the family together and "open their mouth wide," and since God has called me to lead my family, this somebody is me. The only wrong way to have family worship is not to start. May God help us to begin and then continue to assist us when we are tempted to falter.

"The greatest gift a church can receive is to have a group of families who take their responsibilities with such Christian seriousness that they are willing to completely alter their lifestyle to raise up disciples for Jesus Christ." Abraham Kuyper

QUESTIONS FOR REFLECTION

1. What would need to happen for your family to begin meeting and reading scripture together?

2. When is the best time to begin?

3. If you were to choose one time to start small and try having a time of family worship once a week or month, when would it be?

Ingredient 17: God is on Your Team

Next to Isaiah 54:13 in the margin of my Bible I have printed one word: gerbils. Let me give a little background first. In the year after our son John was born with Down Syndrome, we spent many weeks in the hospital working to keep him alive. He had a close call with a virus which put him in an oxygen tent when he was four months old. While he was there, the doctors detected a heart problem which led to two catheterizations at six and eight months, followed by open heart surgery. Two months later a blockage showed up which resulted in intestinal surgery. As a result, Sandi and I both burned out. I was emotionally fried, and Sandi contracted Epstein-Barr, candida, and chronic fatigue. Looking to regroup as a family, we moved to a different state.

The next year we found ourselves in a small ranch home beginning to rebuild but still with health issues and regular battles with fatigue. The boys were looking for a pet, but the options were limited due to my allergies, so we decided on gerbils. Sandi was not enthusiastic at the prospect of these rodents multiplying, escaping from the cage, and taking up housekeeping in our couch and furniture. The pet shop owner was strictly charged to find two male gerbils, which were named Jim Thorpe (my favorite athlete) and Georgie Russell (of Davy Crockett fame).

Within a few weeks, Sandi was teaching the two older boys using a unit study method. The topic this week was related to reproduction. Usually she would have a catchy hands-on illustration to introduce the new unit, but since she was virtually bedridden with her health issues, she covered the basics, handed out the assignments, and rested. You can probably guess what happened. The next morning the boys awoke rejoicing to find a cage full of baby gerbils.

Jim Thorpe was renamed Jemima as she was obviously the mother, and my prophetic wife's fear had come to pass. But I was encouraged. God used this litter of rodents to make me know He was on our team. He looked down from heaven, saw we needed an illustration, and whamo! (a divine creative act), gerbils appeared. Through this experience, God made me know He was alive, He loved our kids more than we did, and He was overseeing their education, even when we were limited physically. My wife was like the woman who anointed Jesus, of whom Jesus said, "She has done what she could." God was there to make up the difference.

Whenever I read Isaiah 54:13—"all your children shall be taught by the lord, and great shall be the peace of your children" —I remember the gerbils. I am reminded that God is alive and desires to see our children gathered around the throne more than we do. He wants them to learn his word and his ways and is intimately involved in their upbringing. As his earthly representatives, God has designed us to pass on eternal truth to our children, but he is working as well. God and willing parents make a great team.

QUESTIONS FOR REFLECTION

1. What was your first "Big Rock" on p. 9?

2. Can you recall an experience when you sensed God was intervening on behalf of your family?

3. What was your number one Big Rock from the first section in the beginning of the book?

POTENTIAL OBSTACLES

Here are a few obstacles I had to overcome, which might also be hurdles for you.

1. Not Modeled

When I speak to parents, I often begin by asking how many people in the room grew up in a family where their parents intentionally taught them the Word of God. I rarely get more than two or three out of 100 who raise their hands. My folks didn't intentionally teach me the Bible. The only times I saw families worshiping together were when I was visiting other families.

We emulate our parents more than we know. When family worship has not been imprinted on our lives, it takes more energy to begin making this a part of the fabric of our own homes. However, God is faithful, and I meet more and more people who are beginning to meet together as families and have seen the transformation in their homes. I have added a section later in this book of accounts of parents who have read this book and been encouraged to start afresh. I hope their stories will encourage you.

2. Expertitis

We live in a culture governed by qualifications. You're not an expert unless you have taken accredited classes, received specific training, or earned a degree. My brother used to teach and provide certification to mechanical contractors. He was one of the experts in his state. When he moved to another state which required "credentials," he was not able to be certified himself. He was the certifier in one state but not qualified in another.

Let's dispose of this myth of credentials. How many of you have ever taught a Sunday School class? How many of you have ever led a youth group devotion? How about Vacation Bible School? A counselor at a summer camp? It seems to me we're all qualified to teach everybody else's kids but not our own. I've asked audiences these questions, and the vast majority of hands indicate most parents have participated in one or more of these activities.

This is a funny thing in our culture. We even go to training on how to become a Sunday School teacher, but when it comes to teaching our own children, we say, "Hey, I'm not qualified." I believe we are more qualified than we think because God created and designed parents to do this very thing. According to His inspired Word, parents are called to teach their children, and when God calls us to do something, He equips us to do it. This is the way He operates.

There is so much potential in the Christian home because after we have taught the Word, we have the unique opportunity to show our students how to live it out in real life. Think of it as having our Sunday School class living with us, or our youth group accompanying us in the car as we do errands. We are the first Christians our children see in action. Our home is their first church.

This arrangement of having our students with us 24/7 is a two-edged sword because we have several pairs of eyes giving us accountability. Not only do the students benefit, but the teacher does as well. We have the added incentive to be more consistent in our walk with God. This is part of the beauty of the Christian home. We stimulate one another to love and good works. We help each other to be doers of the Word and not hearers only. It is such a great idea and an effective model, it must have been designed by God Himself.

Mom the Expert

Dr. Leila Denmark is a legend in the Atlanta area and was our pediatrician for several years. She passed on at the age of 114 in 2012. She was in her eighties when we knew her. Sandi and I followed much of her advice and highly recommend her book *Every Child Should Have A Chance,* published in 1971 by Vantage Press in New York.

Dr. Denmark told me there was a time when doctors would come to your home and say, "Mom, what do you think we have here?" This wise doctor recognized no one knew the child better than the mom. Even though the doctor had some medical expertise and was keeping up-to-date with studies and the latest research, she knew Mom was qualified as well. How times have changed!

Church and the Home

I was in a training session for Sunday School superintendents in our denomination when it was announced a packet of material from Child Evangelism Fellowship on how to lead children to Christ was being made available to all the Sunday School teachers. I raised my hand and asked, "Is there any way we could make these materials available to the parents?"

The room became real quiet, my question was not answered, and the instructor went to the next item on the meeting agenda.

We need to figure out a way for churches and homes to work together. I would like to have someone teach me how to recognize when my children are getting close to receiving Christ. I would welcome input on how to lead worship in my home.

Unfortunately, I am observing a disturbing trend in many churches which gives lip service to the role of parents but, in practice, replaces them. Instead of supporting Dad and Mom, they are supplanting them.

A Winning Combination

When Joe was a young pup in Sunday School class, his teacher recognized he had been particularly sensitive to the things of God this Sunday morning. Instead of taking her packet out and leading him to Christ after class, she went to his parents and said, "I think Joe is close to the Kingdom." So Joe's parents went home, sat him on the bed between them, and explained the gospel to him. Soon all three were kneeling by the bedside, and Joe received Jesus as his personal savior. He's been following Jesus ever since, has been a pastor for many years, and served as my principal when I was a teacher at a Christian school.

That is a neat working relationship between the church and the home. The Sunday School teacher recognizes she is able to use her gifts as a teacher and employs those gifts to support the parents in helping them to do what God has called them to do.

3. Religious Instruction Is the Job of the Church

In 1780, Robert Raikes started the first Sunday school. As the social-minded editor of a newspaper, he was trying to fight poverty and improve the living conditions of the children in the UK who were working long shifts, six days a week, and had no way to get out of their hopeless lifestyle. He came up with the idea of hiring moms in the community to open their homes one day a week, give the children a meal, and teach them how to read, write, and do sums. He hoped if they acquired an education they might break out of the cycle of despair.

What day of the week do you think they chose for the schools? Sunday. Hence the name "Sunday Schools." Later, the church got involved and supported the effort, but it was never meant to become a discipleship experience for children in the church; it was an outreach for children who were not in the church. Sunday Schools were designed to help poor children receive the skills necessary to break free from the cycle of poverty.

"He established a testimony in Jacob and appointed a law in Israel, which he commanded our fathers to teach to their children, that the next generation might know them, the children yet unborn, and arise and tell them to their children, so that they should set their hope in God and not forget the works of God, but keep his commandments." (Psalms 78:5-7)

I first read about Robert Raikes in *The 100 Most Important Events in Christian History*, by A. Kenneth Curtis, Randy Petersen, and J. Stephen Lang, published in 1991 by Christian History Institute. For more information, there is a one hour talk I have presented concerning "Youth Groups and Sunday Schools" on my web site at www.buildingfaithfamilies.org.

4. My Plate Is Already Full

The biggest obstacle for me was the lack of energy to do one more thing. When the boys were all between 4 and 11 years old, we had bought a big unfinished house. Only about half of the home had drywall on the walls, there was almost no flooring, nor was there a heating system, or any landscaping. This was our first home and all we could afford.

It took my boys and me six years to finish it, so I didn't have a lot of extra energy. Now maybe you're not in this particular circumstance, but according to recent data, the number of hours the average worker puts into a week has increased dramatically in recent years. At this time in my life, I thought to myself, "Now I need to add having family devotions." All I could think of was this was one more item on my plate which was already full.

I decided to go ahead and give it a shot anyway, fully expecting to watch more of my limited energy drain out of me, but, unexpectedly, I found life. This little unlooked-for spring of living water sprang up in our home. This is just what Jesus promised.

"Give, and it will be given to you. Good measure, pressed down, shaken together, running over, will be put into your lap." (Luke 6:38)

This experience reminded me of Samson when he took the jawbone of a donkey and slew a thousand Philistines in Judges 15. "And he was very thirsty, and he called upon the LORD and said, 'You have granted this great salvation by the hand of your servant, and shall I now die of thirst and fall into the hands of the uncircumcised?' And God split open the hollow place that is at Lehi, and water came out from it. And when he drank, his spirit returned, and he revived. Therefore the name of it was called En-hakkore; it is at Lehi to this day." (Judges 15:18-19) En-hakkore means "the Spring of the One Who Cried Out."

This precious gathering of our family became a sweet time when God met with us and fed us from His Word. I have read my Bible from Genesis to Revelation many times in my personal devotions, but when I am reading the Word of God with other believers and having Jesus teach us by His Spirit, I see new things, I hear new things, and I gain new insights which I had never received in reading the Bible by myself. Our family worship times have not been a drain on my energy reserves but an unexpected source of living water.

5. Fear

Another obstacle might be the fear of speaking in public. According to pollsters, people would rather die than speak in public. Public speaking and fear of failure are usually listed as the number 1 and number 2 on the list of things people are fearful of doing, in some of the research I have seen. Dying is listed as number 4 or 5 on the list. Do the math. I also think what makes fear of failure right behind speaking in public is because you have the potential to fail in front of other people when you speak.

I don't believe God is calling us to deliver sermons. He is calling us to lead our families. He wants us to be faithful facilitators, not successful sermonizers. When two or three are gathered together in His name, He will show up. Do you think Jesus wants to teach your kids the Bible? Do you think He wants them to understand it? Absolutely! He is also on your team.

Have you ever spoken to your fellow church members after a service? Have you noticed each individual seemed to learn something different than the others, even though they were in the same meeting listening to the same speaker? What does this tell you? God's Spirit was there, and He was able to take the Scripture and adapt it to the unique needs of everyone in the room. Remember the interaction Jesus and Peter had on the mountain:

"Simon Peter replied, 'You are the Christ, the Son of the living God.' And Jesus answered him, 'Blessed are you, Simon Bar-jonah! For flesh and blood has not revealed this to you, but my Father who is in heaven.'" (Matthew 16:16-17)

God knows how to teach people. He's got great ideas. He knows everybody in the class and has invested His life to see they spend eternity with Him. Gather the family together, ask God to join you, and sit back and watch God do wonderful things in your home.

6. Not Qualified

You don't have to be the perfect teacher to read the Bible with your family. Children don't expect parents to be perfect, but they do hope they will be real. As parents, I hope we are willing to learn along with our children, ask for prayer when we need help, and share what God is teaching us as we learn from His Word. Our willingness to be discipled along with the kids can be a huge encouragement to them as they also struggle to grow in the Lord. We have the advantage of having followed Jesus longer than they have. They have the benefit of learning the Word of God from their childhood. Allow me to illustrate how smart our children are.

"He has not beheld iniquity in Jacob, neither has he seen perverseness in Israel." (Numbers 23:21 KJV)

Every time I read this verse I wondered how it could be so. After all, the Israelites were a sinful and rebellious people. I had just finished reading Exodus, Leviticus, and half of Numbers. I puzzled over this particular verse for over fifteen years. When I read Scripture and come to a passage I don't readily understand, I file it away in my mind and figure God is smarter than I am and hope someday I will be able to understand it. Finally after all those years, as I was reading this passage, the light shone in my mind, and I finally comprehended how this Scripture could be true.

It so happened we were about to read Numbers 23 as a family, and I looked forward to being able to explain this difficult passage. After we read the chapter I asked if anyone knew how the Holy Spirit through Balaam could make this statement about the children of Israel. Ethan raised his hand and said, "Well, they had been offering the sacrifices daily in the tabernacle." My shoulders sagged inwardly as my bubble had been burst. He was correct. My seminary-trained mind had taken fifteen years to understand what this stripling grasped in one reading.

So we learn together and we learn from each other. It is how God designed families to operate.

7. Success

We all like to be successful. We like to win. I don't enjoy playing a game unless I can be competitive. I fantasize I can still play some basketball. In my mind, I still have the skills. When I set out to do a job, I want to do it reasonably well. I want, and even need, to succeed. I don't think it is wrong to want to do well and even be "number one." When Jesus was speaking with His disciples, He found them arguing about who was the greatest. Instead of rebuking them for how they were wired, He redirected their ambition.

"Whoever would be great among you must be your servant." (Matthew 20:26)

God defines success differently than the world. In the divine economy, a faithful man is a successful man. We are called to be faithful.

"It is required of stewards that they be found faithful." (1 Corinthians 4:2)

If you are tempted to say, "I'm not a good speaker or even a good facilitator," remember the call of God to our hearts is to sow the seeds faithfully and trust Him to give the increase.

"I planted, Apollos watered, but God gave the growth. So neither he who plants nor he who waters is anything, but only God who gives the growth." (1 Corinthians 3:6–7)

8. Dad's Involvement

The hardest question I am asked is what a husband or wife should do if their spouse is unwilling to participate in the biblical instruction of their children or is indifferent. I do not have a pat answer, but here are some thoughts. First pray that God would turn their heart toward your children. He is able.

"He will turn the hearts of fathers to their children and the hearts of children to their fathers." (Malachi 4:6)

If I were the person in question, I would hope that Sandi could approach me one-on-one and express her desire to have devotions and communicate her burden to me. Even when we weren't meeting as a family in our home, I knew deep down in my heart of hearts it was my responsibility to teach the Word of God to my kids. A godly appeal goes a long way.

What doesn't work is dripping, nagging, or criticizing.

"A continual dripping on a rainy day and a quarrelsome wife are alike; to restrain her is to restrain the wind or to grasp oil in one's right hand." (Proverbs 27:15-16)

Comparing doesn't work either. Try to avoid, "Why can't you be like James Dobson?" Instead, consider this approach: "I have a burden that we teach our children the Bible. Could you pray with me about this?" If they still resist, ask if they would give their blessing for you to teach the kids.

I know of situations where the husband is just plain overworked. Perhaps the wife could read the Word during the day, and Dad could follow up with questions around the dinner table to support and reinforce what Mom taught in the morning.

The life of Timothy gives us hope even when a spouse is not supportive. We don't know whether Timothy's father was a believer in Jesus, but he doesn't appear to be in Acts 16.

"Paul came also to Derbe and to Lystra. A disciple was there, named Timothy, the son of a Jewish woman who was a believer, but his father was a Greek." (Acts 16:1)

We do know his mother and grandmother possessed a sincere faith and passed that on to Timothy. God's Word certainly gives hope to a believing parent.

"I am reminded of your sincere faith, a faith that dwelt first in your grandmother Lois and your mother Eunice and now, I am sure, dwells in you as well." (2 Timothy 1:5)

"To Timothy, my true child in the faith." (1 Timothy 1:2)

When the husband and wife are on the same page in teaching and discipling the children I think you an ideal family situation.

"That the leaders took the lead in Israel, that the people offered themselves willingly, bless the LORD!" (Judges 5:2)

9. Moses

To wrap up this section on potential obstacles, think about Moses, who considered himself unqualified and unprepared. In Exodus 3 and 4, we have a detailed account of the conversation between God and Moses. Moses didn't feel able to lead the people of Israel out of Egypt. He was frank about his perception of his inabilities. Moses' objections were, "Who am I? They will not believe me. I am not eloquent."

As I reread this debate recently, I noticed God was not displeased with the questions. He patiently answered each one with a reminder of who He was and what He would do for him. In this discussion Moses came away with a greater understanding of God's abilities and power than before. It is only when he says, "Let someone else do it" when God gets angry.

"Moses: 'Oh, my Lord, please send someone else'" (Exodus 4:13)

"Then the anger of the LORD was kindled against Moses." (Exodus 4:14)

From our perspective, we know Moses was uniquely qualified to do exactly what God had called him to do. His education in Egypt, coupled with a strong levitical heritage, seasoned by forty years in the wilderness, and enhanced by his experience as a shepherd, made for a peerless candidate who could and would lead the children of Israel out of the wilderness and into the Promised Land.

I believe God has uniquely equipped us to teach our children. You and I were created before the foundation of the world for this very work. This good work. The eternal work of training, teaching, shepherding, and raising our children to live forever with Jesus.

"For we are His workmanship, created in Christ Jesus for good works, which God prepared beforehand, that we should walk in them." (Ephesians 2:10)

WHAT OTHER FAMILIES HAVE DONE

Draw a Picture

Friends from Massachusetts gave each of their children a 4" by 6" white note card to draw a picture of the chapter their dad was reading each day. Their work was displayed hanging from clothespins in their kitchen. I have seen hundreds of colorful "scripture illustrations" hanging from cords on their ceiling.

Act It Out

A family with expressive children came up with a different strategy. After the Bible reading, off go the kids to another room to plan a skit. They then entertain the parents with their homespun production.

B-B-B-B-B

Bath, Brush (teeth), Bible, Bed, Blessings!
This family used the Bible time as an incentive to get their kiddos to bed in a timely fashion. No Bible until bath and brush were accomplished.

Teaching in Texas

By God's grace, a Godly man and mentor, shared Psalm 78:1-8 with me many years ago and exhorted me to teach the Scriptures to my four sons every day. He said, "If we, as fathers, don't honor the Lord daily with our prayers and thanksgiving and if we fail to teach the Scriptures, then we are silently telling our children God is NOT a PART of our daily lives."

Because this is a commandment from God, I made this task a priority and tried my best to faithfully teach the Scriptures every morning to my wife and to my four sons.

I did use one little teaching help, "Teaching the Word of Truth" by Donald G. Barnhouse, but most of the time, I simply taught verse by verse, chapter by chapter through the Bible. I would skip around, an Old Testament book, then several New Testament books, and so on, but tried to teach an entire book before moving on.

We would spend about 15 to 20 minutes a day, opening with prayer first, then reading from the chapter at hand, explaining what God was telling us, then discussing the text among the family. I tried to tie the text into object lessons that were going on in our family so the kids would see the Word of God was not just a collection of ancient writings, but as 2 Timothy 3:16 tells us, it is, "Given by inspiration of God, and is profitable for doctrine, for reproof, for correction, for instruction in righteousness." We would sing a hymn and a praise song, and end in prayer.

I cannot tell you what a sense of accomplishment I feel today when I open my Bible in church on a Sunday morning and see the initials, "FBS 7-11-88" next to a passage of Scripture. I jotted in the margin before every Family Bible Study we had "FBS" and the date we read the passage. I now carry to church, not only the inspired Word of God, but also a record and a history of one less-than-perfect dad who tried in his own feeble way to honor the commandment to, "Teach the wonders and works of God to the next generation!".

Show Me in Missouri

I prayed for God to show me how to be more of a spiritual leader with my kids. Since I didn't really have it modeled and the expectation of what I thought it looked like didn't seem to work every time I tried it, I grew frustrated. But I kept asking God what I could do and thought about what I would want my father to do. I decided interactive games and role playing might be good.

We read one Bible story per night then choose animals or dolls to act out the story. Usually I am the actor, but when the kids know the story really well I ask them if they want to play a part. It amazes me how much they remember and what great questions these "shows" raise. They beg for it each night. "Seeing" what Jesus went through for them on the cross was particularly impactful. And giving them the opportunity to take a stand, for example when they are Shadrach, Meshach and Abednego facing the king and the furnace was particularly encouraging.

Liturgy and Structure

We have four children from 5 to 11. Although the form and length of devotions has changed a lot over the years, we have always tried to make it a time to model our faith, help them become familiar with components of Sunday worship (Apostles' Creed, Gloria Patri, hymns), and mentor them in prayer, worship, and Bible study.

After dinner we gather in the living room. Each child is responsible for a part of the service; prayer, Bible reading, choosing a hymn, or reading a selection. A selection might be a Psalm, Proverb, the Lord's

Prayer, Gloria Patri, or Apostles' Creed. These rotate each week.

Our times take anywhere from 30 to 50 minutes. Our kids generally enjoy devotions and protest if they are ever canceled. It's been a joy to see our kids grow. I especially love to hear them humming hymns as they are doing their schoolwork or playing.

It's Never Too Late

In 1808, Noah Webster was 49. The following two paragraphs are taken from a longer biography entitled *The Life and Testimony of Noah Webster*.

"He had now to decide not only for himself, but, to a certain extent, for others, whose spiritual interests were committed to his charge. Under a sense of this responsibility, he took up the study of the Bible with painful solicitude. As he advanced, the objections which he had formerly entertained against the humbling doctrines of the gospel were wholly removed. He felt their truth in his own experience. He felt that salvation must be wholly of grace. He felt constrained, as he afterward told a friend, to cast himself down before God, confess his sins, implore pardon through the merits of the Redeemer, and there make his vows of entire obedience to the commands and devotion to the service of his maker.

"With his characteristic promptitude, he instantly made known to his family the feelings which he entertained. He called them together the next morning, and told them, with deep emotion, that, while he had aimed at the faithful discharge of all his duties as their parent and head, he had neglected one of the most important, that of family prayer. After reading from the scriptures, he led them with deep solemnity to the throne of grace, and from that time continued the practice, with the liveliest interest, to the period of his death (35 years later)."

So wrote Chauncey A. Goodrich, professor at Yale College, in August 1847. (This is quoted in *Teaching and Learning America's Christian History* by Rosalie Slater published in 1965 by the Foundation for American Christian Education, San Francisco, CA.)

Truth Illustrated

Wow, what a rich time we have been having. We start the day by reading the Proverb for that day and the girls pick a verse they want to illustrate by drawing and coloring a picture. Then I reread the Proverb and we try to guess which verse they drew. They are putting them in one of those spiral notebooks that are blank on the top of the page for drawing and lined on the bottom of the page. I have them write out the verse at the bottom after we guess it. They take such delight and giggle themselves crazy while drawing and guessing.

Then at night as a family, Dave reads the Bible in a Year Old and New Testament and we take our time interrupting him with many questions and comments. Love to see the "aha, light bulb" going off in their heads.

Priority

My husband took over my father's business in the last year, and that has required a lot of overtime and late nights. We always thought we couldn't fit Bible time in every night. I would just put the kids to bed myself and try to wait up to see my husband.

Sometimes several days would go by where they never saw their Dad, as he left before they were awake and returned once they were in bed.

Making this priority to be in God's Word everyday has meant that I have had to budge on structure and schedule, letting the children stay up late on the few occasions Dad has been late. We are finding Dad's leadership strengthened as we wait for him to instruct us each day, and I know that at least one time each day, we will all be going the same direction.

Huge payoff moment this fall when Isabella was baptized. Pastor asked her when she was saved and she told everyone it was after Family Bible time as if everyone had that. Pastor then encouraged all the families to make it part of their home. :)

G-Rated

We are reading through the *One Year Bible* with the kids. It sure does make for some interesting conversations as Genesis is not particularly G rated! People have asked us what we've done to keep it interesting for the kids, but they have really liked it. I will confess to adding voices though. It's pretty funny to read Jacob's words with a thick Texan accent! In the past we've read them Bible stories, but now we read the actual Bible each day.

Jesus Time

We have had a few occasions where we were not at home during our usual Family Bible time, we were at a friends house, and it did NOT deter us. In, fact we got to share this beauty with another family in Christ! We simply had Jesus time with them, one time I got my daughter and the other families daughter to lead our time together... it was priceless!

'Votions

Every evening we read stories directly out of the Bible, with everyone reading the part of a different character (Narrator, Jesus, Mary, etc.). Then one of us leads in prayer, then hugs and kisses and to bed.

Both of our girls love to play the parts (9 and 5 years old). The five year old can't read, but we choose a small part and coach her on what to say. Our five year old also loves to lead in prayer! It doesn't always make sense (she has quite the imagination), but it is fun hearing what she is thinking about! We have had cousins (from a non-christian family) stay the night and they absolutely loved "votions" (as one of them called it).

When we started, it was very hit and miss, but our motto was try, try again. It also really helps when the kids get excited about it. They don't let you slack! We have gotten home late from an event before, where we had to carry the kids in because they fell asleep in the car, and as we were laying them in bed, they stirred and said, "We haven't had devotions yet!"

Not only does it add to the spiritual dynamics of the family, but it adds to the bonding of the family.

Dead Tired

Three years ago while studying and memorizing the 10 commandments, my two oldest were saved. Last month after our time of prayer at the end of our devotion time our 4 year old was broken and full of tears. We finally realized he wanted to ask the Lord into his heart. With laughter and joy he sat on his daddy's lap and accepted Jesus in his heart then promptly told mama to write it down on her chalkboard. Did devotions make a difference? I think so.

1. I think they should be daddy led! It makes it seem more important to them.
2. Both parents should be there if at all possible.
3. Constancy is HUGE—they never ask if we are doing devotions because that is a silly question.

We are often dead tired by the time we get to devotions but they go on. Our biggest struggle is "WHO GETS TO SIT BY DADDY???" There are things we could do better or spend more time on but beating ourselves up over it doesn't help anything. We are committed to doing devotions!

Angels Rejoicing

We had Bible Time everyday for the past 40 days. This is something we had not done in the past. We are so grateful for this challenge. On day 39 all 4 of our daughters gave their lives to Jesus. We plan to continue to meet every night for family Bible Time.

Adapting

At first we were very regimented about everyone gathering around and Dad reading from the Bible but now our Family Devotion Time has evolved as our children are growing older. Most of the time Dad will read from the Bible, *Our Daily Bread, or Jesus Calling.* Sometimes: one of the older children will share a verse or passage that they have studying, and we discuss it. Or Mom will share something that God has impressed upon her.

We read a psalm and then do lots of prayers for family and friends. My youngest will read a verse from his children's Bible to all of us and pray for us. We sing lots of hymns and songs. Somedays we work on memorizing a verse or passage together.

Trying

We clearly are not role models, but we are trying. What we do is to have devotionals at dinner or shortly thereafter, about 6 days a week. We either talk at the table or in the living room. We take turns leading. I still take the lead on getting it started and keeping it focused, but each of us gets to pick the topic and ask the questions, and my son really likes having his turn.

I have been doing lessons on one commandment at a time, reading from Scripture and some good commentaries, while discussing Ray Comfort's use of the 10 Commandments to reach the unsaved. My wife usually reads from her Bible Study Fellowship lesson, which is on the Gospel of Matthew this year. My son uses his *Adventures in Odyssey* devotional book which is specifically designed to be done during a meal. Letting children have an active role is important so it isn't a sermon.

Praying

After praying, we take turns reading the Bible. First dad reads then mom reads. Then we talk about it, sing a hymn, and act out what we read. We also draw pictures of a key verse.

Music helps us gather and settle back from the activities of the day. We all sing two to three hymns using hymnals. We have been reading from a devotional on the names of Jesus, so one of our children reads from that each evening. I usually pray and then we read a section of scripture taking turns from evening to evening.

We close in prayer either with everyone praying out loud or sometimes I pray for us all. We believe children learning to pray out loud in a safe environment is important. It also helps us understand what they are concerned about and sometimes we are surprised by their depth of understanding and sensitivity in the prayers they offer up to God.

Determined

We have struggled with being consistent with our family devotions for many years now. When you introduced this contest it gave us some motivation to try a little harder. The 1st year, we failed miserably. The 2nd year was a little better, but once again I allowed my schedule to take priority in my life. In the 3rd year, with encouragement from my wife, we started family devotions again with a new outlook. By Jan 1, 2014, we had already been doing Family Devotions and were even more determined to stick with the contest.

A few weeks ago, we realized we had finally done it, we had succeeded in making it a habit for the whole family! We also realized that the contest was no longer our motivation, but instead, our motivation comes from the Lord and seeing our children grow in the knowledge of Christ!

Every night before bed, our children habitually gather around the living room and listen to me read the Bible. They are then allowed to ask questions about what we read, or we discuss it deeper. After that, our children take turns praying. We have used that time to pray for the needs of others and have learned some hard lessons over the last few months about life.

Thankful Wife

We attended one of your workshops at the conference. We also picked up one of your books for the family devotion challenge. I'm happy to report that we have been doing family devotions every day after dinner. Right after we eat we read a chapter. We also started in Genesis as your book suggested. My husband has never been one to do this before, I'm very thankful that we are finally doing it together.

30 DAY CHALLENGE

During the conference season I like to challenge parents to read this book within one month of taking it home. If they do, they can keep the book for free; if not, they send a check to Building Faith Families. Thirty days later I send an e-mail asking whether they have read the book in the allotted time frame, if they have attempted having a family worship time, and what were their chief takeaways from the book. I've had the privilege of reading through hundreds of responses and have selected a few to give you a flavor of this treasure trove of heartfelt emails. As you read their words, you will see that God is alive and working in the hearts of these parents, for they are kindred spirits who are committed to God and their families.

For those of you reading this book for the first time, I believe God is already working in your heart or you would not have read this far. In Malachi 4, we read of God turning the hearts of fathers to their children and vice versa. This good work of teaching our children the eternal Word of God is a part of that moving of the Spirit in our day. Kudos to you. Keep up the God work, for we shall certainly reap eternal fruit if we faint not.

Our Responsibility

As soon as I finished the Big Rocks section (twice) and half way through the Family Worship chapters, my wife and I started our Family Worship with my son.

I learned that teaching him about God and His laws is my responsibility (not the church or Sunday School teacher). Your book is very helpful on how to conduct

Family Worship and It is much easier and simpler than I thought.

Chief Takeaways

1 – It is never too late to start.
2 – Let the kids know of the "scheduled" time for family worship. This helps to manage their expectations.
3 – Let the kids participate at their level. (I can get impatient with slow readers.)

We have been doing family worship once a week. We are planning on increasing to twice a week in July.

I did not grow up in a Christian household. Family Worship still feels like a forced event. I believe the level of my personal worship time will enhance the level of my family worship time.

Relax

Since reading this book, I have changed our "schedule" and mixed it up a little bit. I still do it at night time at times but I choose something that will not require them to sit for too long. I have also had bible time on the trampoline, under the tree in the backyard or right after dinner (which seems to be the best time when I am home).

I have realized that I need to RELAX. I have been letting the kids be more wiggly and even have a quiet toy during our time. I have found that my kids love to act out the story we just read and get real animated with it, so this has also been a good addition to our time. Letting go of my expectations has been huge for me and has really lifted a burden off of my back.

Servant Leader

I liked the part on "just do it" and to not get discouraged. Another thing is the need to be a servant leader. I can get demanding thereby provoking my children to anger. So I want to be able to fulfill my duty, but do it with love and care.

Sharing Stories

There were many parts that really stuck with me but one that hit me the most was sharing my personal experiences with my kids. I felt bad that I haven't. I do have many stories where God has touched my life.

Happy Kids

For six months we have read scripture and discussed it every evening immediately after we are finished dinner. We have 3 boys, 21, 19, 13. They have all shown enthusiasm towards the our new time together with God. This totally caught me off guard. I knew they would be respectful and participate. I just didn't know they would show appreciation so soon.

Ears to Hear

My chief takeaway from the book was that I need to let other's have input concerning our devotion time. I have a strong take charge mindset, and of course I thought I knew what everyone needed. Sometimes my wife may be dealing with different issues, needing something different on a given day than what "I think" she needs.

I ultimately lead the worship time but having input and conversations with my wife and her daily observance as to what the children may be dealing with has opened up a more interactive worship time with the family.

Setting the Table

The main thing I took away from it was sort of like the Nike slogan: "Just do it." So I did. We read usually at dinner time, and although it's not every day, like you say in the book it's more than we have been doing. We have gotten up through Genesis 17, and I ask them questions after the reading is done.

It has an effect, too. We have daily tasks for our children, one of which is setting the table. The child whose turn it is to set the table also gets to choose who sits where, giving them all a chance to sit by Mommy. My middle son has started marking my place at the dinner table by setting the Bible on my plate. If I don't read he is the one to remind us all. I may never have known how much he enjoys hearing the Word of God if I had not not begun.

Failing Forward

YES!!! I was able to read the book well within the allotted time frame. One of the things that spoke most profoundly to me was "just start" for anything is better than the nothing that was happening. We had started devotions MANY times and for various reasons always fell off track. With a perfectionist mindset; it was not easy for me to 'fail', however, I came to realize that as long as we try we are 'failing forward' and that is greater than failing in the same place.

Family Discipleship

I finished reading the book one day before the deadline. It gave us encouragement, as we struggle to keep the discipline of having daily devotions. The outcome is that my husband bought the ESV Daily Reading Bible for every member of our crew! :) It has been a blessing, and the goal is to read the Bible in one year. Every day we read 4 chapters, which come already in the right sequence, i.e. DAY 1: Genesis 1, Matthew 1 (read aloud by every member of the family) and Ezra 1, Acts 1, silent reading, although we remain together during that period. When everybody is ready, we pray, sing a hymn and work in the memorization of a Bible passage (a passage per week).

Family Culture

Well, I'm aware that the family worship challenge was put forth mainly to the men but I signed up knowing that my husband who was absent would appreciate it. We finished the book by reading it aloud to each other on a road trip. We appreciated all the anecdotes of yours and others' family worship experiences. We gleaned some good ideas to freshen up our family worship experience. You're preaching to the choir with us. We have been doing family worship daily ever since we've been married. It has taken on different flavors and styles along the way as our 3 kids are growing up. We've known the blessing of the family culture that ensues and the joy of covenant living that it fosters.

We've spent several years as missionaries then relocated a year ago and it was a major upheaval. Our family worship became a good time to process with our children, to speak openly of our grief and fears and to debrief along the way. We did not have to create a new forum for this, we already had this time to meet, read scripture and pray and it was natural to just use this time to commit this major transition to the Lord.

Hubby and Wife on the Same Page

I appreciate the challenges and encouragement in the book. My primary take away is to JUST DO IT! and that I don't need special qualifications to be able to read and talk about Gods word with my kiddos. I was feeling frustrated because family devotions weren't happening in our family and I thought they should. The book gave me the courage to have a conversation with my hubby about it and we have decided that I will read in the morning with the kids before we do school and he will read at supper.

Laying Down Life for Family

Thank you for helping/making me read your book. With my wife and you as motivation, I have learned during our nightly bible time with our girls, that I should be taking more of a leadership role and read to my girls instead of letting my wife do it all. I am not a fan of sitting down and reading, but I know this will help out our family.

Well Begun is Half Done

I have finished the book. What's crazy is that I'm a slow reader and I finished it in two settings! The main thing that caught my attention was the idea of allowing everyone to participate in the family worship time. I've already passed the book along to another dad in our church and I'm excited to hear his thoughts. Yes, we have started our family worship and we are loving it!

Chronicles

I finished the book then listened to the audio. I have been a Christian much of my life and raised in a Christian home. But I still had a lot of trouble having family time with God.

As the father I have been inspired to take initiative and put more determination behind our special time with God. We had tried several different times during the day and never found a good time which worked for us. Since reading your book, we have implemented a new policy in our family. For the first time ever we began keeping a daily devotional diary taking turns filling in the diary with each of these specific notations.

1) the date
2) the name of the diary keeper that day
3) the song book and number of the song we sing
4) the passage of Scripture we read
5) something new that he/she learned or that stood out to them inspiring new zeal

This has been enthusiastically carried out by all in the family. From our four teens to mom and dad, we each look forward to our turn filling out the diary. We plan to use it as inspirational memorabilia in the future.

Pass It On

Another Dad had me write in the flyleaf of the book a short sentence and then he wrote numbers down the page. He was going to read the book, sign his name by #1, and then pass it along to other men in his church and ask them to sign their names when they have finished the book.

Out of the Mouth of Babes

My 5 yr old daughter is so observant when my emotions start getting heightened with the kids and she says "mom you should read the bible!" And when we stop to pray and read God's word, she''ll astutely comment, "mom your attitude is so much better after reading the bible!". It's so embarrassing having to be reminded by my 5 year old but I am also thankful God can use my times of weakness to show them how spending time in God's word transforms us. Ah, God's refining fires of marriage and child rearing!

Gaining Confidence

I have had time to read the Family Worship book and have enjoyed it. I would say that it has helped me gain the confidence needed to just start/try doing devotionals every day. I homeschool which SHOULD make it easier to find time to squeeze into our schedule but I found myself being really lazy about it this year. Primarily because even though I was brought up in a Christian home, my brothers and I were never really "taught" about the Bible and scripture as much as we should have been. I felt I was at a loss because I was afraid I was doing doing it wrong...sometimes I struggle with interpreting the Bible myself. Lol After reading your book I now know that there really is NO wrong way to go about this.

It's OK if We Fall

I knew that one of my priorities would be to teach my kids His Word. So we started out the year strong doing devotionals during our school time but after a few months of trying to get a hang of the whole homeschool thing... our devotional time fizzled out.

I have made many other attempts to restart it and be consistent with it... but I seem to always be falling short. Your book gave me the peace and hope in knowing that God has already equipped me to teach my children and if I rely on his strength and not my own... He will provide and help. Also, it helped me to realize that it's ok if we fall... we just need to get right back up and keep at it. "Open your mouth wide an I will it." (Psalm 81:10) "The righteous falls seven times and rises again." (Proverbs 24:16)

I YEARN for my husband to take the lead and be a part of bible time with our family. He works long days, leaves early...gets home late, and I know that he is drained. It's been a struggle for me but you know what... I haven't given it to God! Well, of course I should pray for my husband and for him (and WITH him) to have a heart to want to lead our family!

Recommitted

There really wasn't any earth shattering information in the book that I hadn't heard before but the book really helped bring me back to where I needed to be. My wife and I do devotional times with the kids most evenings but with home schooling and work it doesn't all ways happen. Since reading your book we have been more committed to doing those devotions and the kids have responded positively to that. They will actually beg us to do devotions even when its late and we would rather go to bed.

Encouraged

Thanks for checking in. It's very motivational to know you'll be writing. :-)

I just finished a combo of reading and listening to the book and feel so encouraged. My 4 year old has been listening along with me in the car and keeps asking to listen to "the rocks in the glass book." :-)

One of the most encouraging things to me was realizing that family devotions should be enjoyed and it's okay to be more casual about it...reading while the kids jump, acting out the stories, etc. I grew up in a great Christian home, but honestly, our devotion time was kind of a drudgery. I really appreciated that my parents did this with us, but I never really looked forward to it. I'm hoping my husband and I, with so many useful tips found in your book, will be able to create a time that our boys remember with fondness and look forward to. I know every day won't be like that, but at least a few. :-)

"Just Do It" is also motivational for me. I often want to plan things out and get ready to start before I feel like we'll do a good job; therefore, it never gets done. Just Do It; God will work! We've been waiting for my husband's work schedule to calm down, but it still isn't so we need to quit waiting. 1 minute is better than nothing!

We're looking forward to applying these things this coming month.

For Your Friends

If you would like to offer a 30 Day Challenge or purchase these books in bulk, for parents in your church, small group, or some other kind of fellowship gathering, contact me sdemme@demmelearning.com and we will either work out a special discount price.

APPENDIX

Tips for Teachers

The personality of the leader can set the tone for a family worship time. Much has been written about personalities. Over the years, four main personality characteristics have emerged. I have chosen the D-I-S-C model to distinguish them. Most of us are a blend of these four traits, but I hope these broad strokes will be a helpful introduction to this subject. Recognizing your bent can help you to be more balanced in your approach and teaching style.

D Lion, a Driver, or Choleric. Words to fill out a picture of this type beginning with the letter D are: Dominant, Determined, Doer, Direct, Dogmatic, Demanding, and Decisive.

The "D", who is a take charge leader, may improve his leadership by listening more and asking good questions.

The purpose in a man's heart is like deep water; But a man of understanding will draw it out. Proverbs 20:5

Know this, my beloved brothers: let every person be quick to hear, slow to speak, slow to anger; James 1:19

I An Otter, is Expressive, or Sanguine. Words beginning with I to describe this type are: Inspirational, Influential, Interested in People, Interactive, and Impressive.

The "I" personality has no problem having an entertaining time of fellowship, but could probably improve his presentation by being accurate and stopping and starting in a timely fashion.

I assure you, until heaven and earth disappear, even the smallest detail of God's law will remain until its purpose is achieved. So if you break the smallest commandment and teach others to do the same, you will be the least in the Kingdom of Heaven. But anyone who obeys God's laws and teaches them will be great in the Kingdom of Heaven. Matthew 5:18-19 NLT

But all things should be done decently and in order. 1 Corinthians 14:40

S A Golden Retriever, is Amiable, or Phlegmatic. Words beginning with S to describe this type are: Supportive, Steady, Stable, Sensitive, and Sweet.

The "S", while comfortable with the status quo and the way things have always been, may need to step up to the plate and take the lead.

"Have I not commanded you? Be strong and courageous. Do not be frightened, and do not be dismayed, for the LORD your God is with you wherever you go." Joshua 1:9

For God gave us a spirit not of fear but of power and love and self-control. 2 Timothy 1:7

C   A Beaver, is Analytical, or Melancholy. Words beginning with C to describe this type are: Careful, Cautious, Competent, Contemplative, and Conservative.

The "C" is usually accurate, but might benefit from parables or illustrations to make his meetings more appealing.

All these things Jesus said to the crowds in parables; indeed, he said nothing to them without a parable. Matthew 13:34

For additional information, consider www.personality-insights.com.

There are a few books that have helped me in this area, *"Who Do You Think You Are Anyway"* and *"Different Kids Different Needs,"* both by Robert Rohm.

Find a Good Dictionary

One year I taught fifth and sixth graders in a Christian School. We had morning Bible times and we decided to read the New Testament as a class, one chapter per day. By including weekends and holidays, we read the 260 chapters during the school year. Early on in our reading, students began to tell me they didn't know what several of the words meant. Our school was using the NIV translation at the time. I chose this opportunity to teach vocabulary and spelling and chose one word per chapter for them to look up. They would write the definition in cursive, and use it in a sentence using manuscript. This way we incorporated spelling, vocabulary, and penmanship, and we were developing a better understanding of scripture.

I was surprised to find that many modern dictionaries did not have definitions that accurately convey the meaning of scripture. If you decide to encourage your children to look up words that they don't understand, may I suggest you consider the *"Webster's 1828 Dictionary"* as a resource. Here are examples of the definitions for the word righteousness, one from www.Dictionary.com and the other from the online version of the 1828 Webster's. I think you will see the difference. You can purchase the Webster's 1828 version as a hard bound book or get it in electronic form in several places online.

Righteousness, n. riíchusness. http://www.1828-dictionary.com/

1. Purity of heart and rectitude of life; conformity of heart and life to the divine law. Righteousness, as used in Scripture and theology, in which it is chiefly used, is nearly equivalent to holiness, comprehending holy principles and affections of heart, and conformity of life to the divine law. It includes all we call justice, honesty and virtue, with holy affections; in short, it is true religion.
2. Applied to God, the perfection or holiness of his nature; exact rectitude; faithfulness.
3. The active and passive obedience of Christ, by which the law of God is fulfilled. Daniel 9.
4. Justice; equity between man and man. Luke 1.

5. The cause of our justification. The Lord our righteousness. Jer. 23.

right · eous · ness   [rahy–chuhs–nis]   –n.   <http:// dictionary.reference.com/

1. the quality or state of being righteous.
2. righteous conduct.
3. the quality or state of being just or rightful: They came to realize the righteousness of her position on the matter.

ABOUT THE AUTHOR

Steve Demme and his wife Sandra have been married since 1979. They have been blessed with four sons, three lovely daughters-in-law, and three special grandchildren.

Steve has served in full or part time pastoral ministry for many years after graduating from Gordon-Conwell Theological Seminary. He is the creator of Math-U-See and the founder of Building Faith Families and has served on the board of Joni and Friends, PA.

He produces a monthly newsletter, weekly podcasts, and regular posts https://www.facebook.com/stevedemme/

Steve is a regular speaker at home education conferences, men's ministry events, and family retreats. His desire is to strengthen, teach, encourage, validate, and exhort parents and families to follow the biblical model for the Christian home.

BUILDING FAITH FAMILIES

Exists to teach and encourage families to embrace the biblical model for the Christian home.

Scripture declares God created the sacred institution of the family. In His wisdom, He designed marriage to be between one man and one woman. We believe healthy God-fearing families are the basic building block for the church and society.

The family is foundational and transformational. Parents and children become more like Jesus as they lay their lives down for each other, pray for each other, and learn to love each other as God has loved them.

RESOURCES TO ENCOURAGE AND STRENGTHEN YOUR FAMILY

- The Monthly Newsletter is an encouraging exhortation as well as updates on Bible contests and upcoming speaking engagements.

- Podcast Each week an episode is released on our website, Itunes, and our Facebook page. These may be downloaded for free.

- Seminars for free download For over 20 years Steve has been speaking and teaching at conferences around the world. Many of his messages are available for your edification. .

- Regular Posts on Facebook Like us and receive short uplifting insights from scripture or a biblical exhortation.

www.buildingfaithfamilies.org

HYMNS FOR FAMILY WORSHIP

This time-honored collection of 100 classic hymns will be a rich addition to your family worship. Make a joyful noise to the LORD!

In addition to the music for these carefully selected songs of worship, the history and origin of each hymn enhances the meaning of the lyrics.

There are four CDs with piano accompaniment for singing along in your home, car, or church.

Some of the titles are:

- What a Friend We Have in Jesus
- Holy, Holy, Holy
- It Is Well With My Soul
- To God Be The Glory
- All Hail the Power of Jesus Name
- Amazing Grace
- How Firm a Foundation
- Blessed Assurance
- Christ Arose
- Rise Up O Men of God
- Jesus Paid It All
- Just As I Am, along with 88 more!

STEWARDSHIP

Stewardship is a biblical approach to personal finance. It is appropriate for anyone with a good grasp of basic math and has completed Algebra 1. I wrote this curriculum for a young adult who was thinking about getting a job, purchasing a car, acquiring a credit card, and opening a bank account. It is full of practical application and the principles being taught are from a Christian Worldview. Many parents have commented they wish they had this class when they were a young adult.

Consider Stewardship for individual study, small group discussion, and adult ministries.

Stewardship Instruction Pack
The Stewardship Instruction Pack contains the instruction manual with lesson-by-lesson instructions, detailed solutions, Biblical Foundation, and the DVD with lesson-by-lesson video instruction.

Biblical Foundation
This concise 150 page book has thirty chapters that address a variety of topics for those who would be a faithful steward of God's resources. Steve references over 200 verses from Genesis to Revelation in sharing how God has helped him to apply scripture principles in his home and business. It is included in the Instruction Pack.

STEWARDSHIP

Stewardship Student Pack

The Stewardship Student Pack contains the Student Workbook with lesson–by–lesson worksheets, and review pages. It also includes the Stewardship Tests.

- Earning Money
- Percent
- Taxes
- Banking
- Checking
- Interest
- Investing
- Budgeting
- Percents at the Store
- Credit Cards
- Comparison Shopping
- Cost of Operating an Automobile
- Cost for Owning a Home versus Renting
- Wise Charitable Giving
- Starting Your Own Business, and more

Thanks for this curriculum! This was the best math course I've taken in all my high school years, and I don't even like math :)
                              - Caleb

That your curriculum is Christ-centered has made the biggest difference in my homeschool experience.
                              - Sarah

My family and I just finished the Stewardship course. Thank you for another great Math-U-See program.
                              - Toby

CRISIS TO CHRIST,

THE HARDEST AND BEST YEAR OF MY LIFE

I have wounds, scars, baggage, and stuff from my past, which I have tried to ignore, but which is always present. In 2012 I was confronted with the distressing knowledge that my own wounds, which I thought were hidden and of no consequence, were wounding those closest to me, my wife and sons. I discovered I cannot hide my toxic issues for eventually they will leak out and hurt those who are closest to me, primarily my wife and children.

This difficult time, the hardest and best year of my life, was instrumental in changing my life and transforming my relationship with God and my family. On this journey I experienced pain which led me to acknowledge my own hurts and get help from the body of Christ to understand root causes of my distress and confront unbiblical thinking.

Crisis to Christ

THE HARDEST AND BEST YEAR OF MY LIFE

STEVE DEMME

While I experienced incredible pain, I also discovered that my Heavenly Dad likes me just the way I am. Even though my path went through deep waters, God was with me every step of the way.

My motivation in writing is to affirm others who are going through similar valleys and tribulations. These hard journeys are normal for the Christian. Every person of note in scripture endured at least one life changing crisis. God uses these difficult times to work deep in our hearts, reveal more of Himself, and transform us into the image of His Son.

KNOWING GOD'S LOVE,

BECOMING ROOTED AND GROUNDED IN GRACE

Comprehending God's unconditional love is the cornerstone for the overarching commands to love God and our neighbor. For we are unable to love until we have first been loved. "We love, because He first loved us." (1 John 4:19) and "In this is love, not that we have loved God but that he loved us." (1 John 4:10)

The first, or as Jesus called it, the Great Command, is to love God. I began asking God to help me love Him with all my heart, soul, mind, and strength and was wonderfully surprised by how he answered my request.

Instead of awaking one morning with a burning love for God, which I expected, He began to steadily reveal how much He loved me. In 2012 I found myself believing in a new way that God knows me thoroughly and loves me completely. This knowledge that God likes me for who I am, and not based on what I do, has transformed my life.

As I have become more rooted and grounded in grace, my relationship with God is now much richer and deeper. My wife and I are closer than we have ever been. Knowing I am loved and accepted just as I am, has freed me to be more transparent and real as I relate with my sons and others.

TRANSFORMED IN LOVE,

LOVING OTHERS AS JESUS HAS LOVED US

John 15:9 revealed God not only loved the world, He loved me. Jesus says to His disciples, "As the Father has loved me, so have I loved you. Abide in my love." Just as the Father loved His Son, Jesus loves me the same way.

The secret to abiding in God's love is found in the next few verses. "If you keep my commandments, you will abide in my love, just as I have kept my Father's commandments and abide in His love. This is my commandment, that you love one another as I have loved you." (John 15:10, 12)

As I love others, as I have been loved, I will abide in the love of God. As a husband and father, my primary responsibilities are to love God, my wife, and my sons. I am writing as a man and sharing how God has led me to begin applying these principles in our home. But these principles are applicable to every believer.

The fruit of loving others as we have been loved will not only bless each of our homes, but our communities as well. "By this all people will know that you are my disciples, if you have love for one another." (John 13:34)

As family members pray for one another, bear each other's burdens, lay their lives down for each other, and learn to love one another as Jesus has loved them, they are transformed and become more like Jesus.

SPEAKING THE TRUTH IN LOVE,

LESSONS I'VE LEARNED ABOUT
FAMILY COMMUNICATION

Most of what I've learned about communication, I acquired in the past few years during transitioning my business to a family owned business. The ability to communicate about difficult topics like business, values, your occupation, and a family's legacy takes effort and training.

As a husband and father, I have the potential to build up and encourage my family like no one else. I also have the ability to tear down and discourage my wife and sons. The Bible teaches effective principles of communication which are timeless.

My relationship with my wife and children has been transformed through godly safe communication. As I continue to grow in grace and the knowledge of God, I am in a better place to have open, transparent, and honest communication. While the skills we have acquired in being a clear speaker and an engaged listener are beneficial, investing time to have a quiet heart is essential. For out of the abundance of the heart, the mouth speaks.

I hope the principles we have learned and applied to such benefit in our own home and business will be a help to you on your journey. May the words of our mouth and the meditation of our heart be acceptable in your sight, O LORD, our Rock and our Redeemer. (from Psalms 19:14)